An Angel Saved Me

True Stories of Divine Intervention

Theresa Cheung

SIMON &
SCHUSTER

London · New York · Sydney · Toronto · New Delhi

A CBS COMPANY

First published in Great Britain by Simon & Schuster UK Ltd, 2011
A CBS COMPANY

1 3 5 7 9 10 8 6 4 2

Simon & Schuster UK Ltd
1st Floor
222 Gray's Inn Road
London WC1X 8HB

www.simonandschuster.co.uk

Simon & Schuster Australia, Sydney
Simon & Schuster India, New Delhi

A CIP catalogue record for this book is available
from the British Library.

ISBN: 978-1-84983-013-3

Typeset in Plantin Light by Hewer Text UK Ltd, Edinburgh
Printed and bound by CPI Group (UK) Ltd, Croydon, CR0 4YY

Contents

Acknowledgements

An Angel Saved Me was only possible because of the support and commitment of some rather wonderful people. I particularly want to thank my agent, Clare Hulton, for her support and belief in my angel books, my editor, Kerri Sharp, for her advice and encouragement, and everyone at Simon and Schuster for being so very helpful throughout the entire process of writing this book and getting it ready for publication.

I'd also like to take this opportunity to thank once again, from the bottom of my heart, everyone who has written to me over the years to share their inspiring angel stories, or to offer me their personal thoughts and spiritual insights. I'm deeply indebted to you all because your stories are the heart and spirit of every angel book I write, and I am convinced that your words are bringing hope and healing to all those who read them.

Special thanks, as always, to Ray, Robert and Ruthie for their love and patience when I went into exile to complete this book. And last, but by no means least, special thanks go to everyone who reads this book. It found its way into your hands for a reason and I hope it will find a home in your heart.

All night, all day, angels watchin' over me, my Lord.

All night, all day, angels watchin' over me.

African-American spiritual

Dear Angel ever at my side,
how lovely you must be—
To leave your home in heaven,
to guard a child like me.
When I'm far away from home,
or maybe hard at play—
I know you will protect me,
from harm along the way.
Your beautiful and shining face,
I see not, though you're near.
The sweetness of your lovely voice,
I cannot really hear.
When I pray, you're praying too,
Your prayer is just for me.
But, when I sleep you never do,
You're watching over me.

Frederick W. Faber

And yet, when I look up at the sky, I somehow feel that everything
will change for the better. That this cruelty too shall end,
that peace and tranquillity will return once more.

Anne Frank

Introduction:
Saved by an Angel

*Miracles . . . seem to me to rest not so much upon faces or voices or
healing power coming suddenly near to us from afar off, but upon
our perceptions being made finer, so that for a moment our eyes can
see and our ears can hear what is there about us always.*

Willa Cather

*Who will tell whether one happy moment of love or the joy of
breathing or walking on a bright morning and smelling the fresh air
is not worth all the suffering and effort which life implies?*

Erich Fromm

Without a doubt angels have saved my life – not once, but
many times.

It used to matter a great deal to me that others believed
my story. That isn't the case today. I'd be lying if I said it
didn't matter at all – as nothing would give me more joy
than to open your mind to the life-changing possibility of
angels – but as each year passes it matters less and less,
because I know it is true. I also know that the angels will
find ways to speak to those who need to hear them, and if

my story isn't the catalyst for belief then perhaps something else will be.

There is, of course, no proof that beings of light are real, just the word of growing numbers of ordinary people, like me, who have experienced them. Even though in the justice system a witness statement is taken as evidence, I'm very aware that this lack of tangible proof remains a source of disbelief, scepticism and frustration for many people; but just because proof of something can't always be presented does not necessarily mean that it is not real. For instance, love is something we can't see but no one doubts that it is real and has the power to transform lives. In much the same way, for those whose lives have been touched by the divine there really is no need for proof or explanation, because there is no doubt. The definition of faith, after all, is to believe without proof, and to those who believe, nothing will ever have as much power as their heartfelt trust and faith in a higher power guiding and protecting them.

Scientists today are also busy discovering and learning about things they believe to be real but cannot prove – curved space, ephemeral matter and liquid time to name a few – and is there a reason why angel experiences should be treated any differently? It could even be said that from a quantum scientist's perspective, encounters with the invisible realm are simply things that we have yet to understand sufficiently. And it seems that our age-old yearning to understand who and what we are by reaching out to the invisible realm for answers isn't fading with the advance of modern science and the relentless march of materialism; it is growing stronger. Indeed, interest in angels has reached fever pitch today with countless books, websites, magazines and societies testifying to that interest.

As if to underline this point, in December 2010, while I was completing this book, newspapers and the internet were reporting that: 'A third of Britons believe an angel is watching over them.' According to this new research, 31 per cent of people believe in angels; a sure-fire sign of the deep spiritual need growing within many of us. And it is abundantly clear that the angels are responding to this growing need. They are hearing our heartfelt cries for salvation. They are making themselves known to us as never before through the stories of ordinary people – people like you and me.

Let's face it, at times we all need to feel we are being watched over. And this was never more true for me than a couple of decades ago when I was a lonely, penniless twenty-something trying to find a place for myself in the world.

The room with no view

A year earlier it had all started so well. I'd left university and got a job at a publishing house working on a subject close to my heart – mind, body and spirit books. I really felt this was the perfect job for me, but a year later the company was taken over and I was offered a small redundancy package. It was a devastating blow. I had to start all over again.

I applied for jobs but with very little work experience there was absolutely no interest. To make matters worse I didn't have anywhere to live. I couldn't live with my boyfriend any more because as soon as I lost my job we broke up, and I couldn't stay with friends because I had lost touch with almost all of them. You see, my ex had been very jealous and possessive and for the past two years it had been just me and him. I couldn't go back home to lick my wounds because there was no home to go to after my mum had died the year before. All that was left from her was debt, and piles and piles of papers, books and other possessions in storage to sort out. When I had a job my life had structure, and I could just about cope financially, but without a job my life fell apart. I was in serious trouble.

So there I was, a jobless, homeless and lonely young woman who felt confused and worthless. With few choices open to me, I used some of the last of my redundancy money to rent a room the size of a broom cupboard in a hostel. In my room with no view there was a single bed, a tiny cupboard and a tiny sink. If I stood up and stretched my arms out to the sides I could almost touch each wall. By far the most depressing thing about it, though, was the smell of dirty laundry that just seemed to be everywhere.

There were three floors to the hostel, eight people to a floor and only one bathroom per floor. On my first night there was a great deal of commotion because a woman living in the room next door to me had overdosed. The following week a middle-aged man who lived in the room opposite was carried out by paramedics in what looked like a black bin bag. I never found out who he was or how he had died. All I can remember is that he was terribly overweight and looked very unhappy whenever I saw him and there was always an aroma of stale fry-ups coming from his room.

Trying to stay positive in such a depressing environment was a real challenge. I knew I had to get out, so I put all my energy into applying for a job. Every day brought rejection after rejection and with my redundancy money fast disappearing I knew it was time to sign on. I never did in the end, though, and not because I didn't want to or need to, but because when I joined the queue at the dole office I was hassled by two guys who had obviously had a lot to drink. They probably were harmless and just as scared and lonely as I was, but I was terrified and didn't dare go back.

I knew that I didn't have the luxury to wait for the kind of publishing job I wanted, so I did anything I could to bring in the cash. I stacked shelves, waitressed, cleaned and did some door-to-door selling on commission. The money I earned was barely enough to pay the rent but it was enough to survive. The touble was that after a few months of this soul-destroying way of life I was permanently hungry and tired. I tried to do some freelance writing but, unable to afford a typewriter, my hand-written features were consistently returned with a polite 'No thank you'. I tried to apply for jobs, but as time wore on my motivation waned and I couldn't see the point of filling out endless application forms any more. Basically, I stopped bothering, stopped caring. I was a bit like a robot. I got up, I worked and I went to sleep. Each day blurred into the next.

It would be an understatement to say that things weren't going well for me. I really needed to believe my angels were watching over me but even that felt unlikely. I didn't see, hear or sense anything. I felt totally alone. I'm ashamed to say that on more than one occasion I did wonder if I might be the next person taken out of the house in a black bin bag. Poverty and loneliness were draining the life out of me. I'd love to say I had the strength of spirit to rise above it all, but I didn't. I wish I could say I found the courage within me to trust in my angels, but again I failed. I was crumbling, fading away into survival mode, and the darkness, cynicism, doubt and despair that kind of existence can bring with it.

And then something remarkable – astonishing even – happened to pull me out of my rut and renew my faith in myself and in my angels as never before. My salvation came from the most unlikely source. It happened, as has often been the case for me, when I woke up one morning with the images of a dream still fresh in my mind. I've always been fascinated by dreams and it was clear that this dream was one I needed to pay attention to because it was so vivid. I can still recall it to this day, twenty-five years later.

In this dream I 'met' a disabled man I used to work for when I was in my late teens and still living at home with Mum. At the time I was trying to home study for my A levels and I did odd jobs, like working as a home help, so I could earn money to help pay the bills. The man was called Mr Rosin and he was someone I very much admired and with whom I had immediately struck up a great rapport. I used to go round to visit him every week to do some light chores, but after a few months the chores became less and less and we would chat more and more. I admired him greatly because all his life he had been severely disabled but this had not stopped him getting qualifications and becoming an inspirational business lecturer at a local college. He used to tell me that he admired my discipline and hard-working approach to life and he was absolutely thrilled for me when, against all the odds and everyone's expectations, including my own, I got a place at Cambridge. He really believed in me. Looking back, with my father absent for much of my childhood, I see he was a kind of father figure for me at the time. He had so many wonderful anecdotes and was always so positive and encouraging. Spending time with him was a pure joy. He made me feel that just about anything was possible. I always left his house feeling better about myself.

Regrettably, I lost touch with him when I went to university and in my second year I found out that he had passed over. At the time it made me sad to think I would not catch up with him again, but I couldn't honestly say that I had thought about him a lot over the years. And yet several years later I had had this vivid dream of him and in my dream he was angry with me. He was telling me to remember who I was, and not to forget the past.

In the days that followed, the dream lingered in my mind. I couldn't let it go and it puzzled and saddened me. Was Mr Rosin angry with me in spirit for losing touch with him? Looking back, it had been rather selfish and thoughtless of me. I guess I had been intoxicated by my first taste of life away from home, but this was just an excuse. I should not have lost touch with him and in my heart I asked him to forgive me.

Or was my dream urging me to discover the inner strength I was clearly lacking? The inner strength, the fighting spirit Mr Rosin had embodied and which he used to say he recognised in me. I started to think about how Mr Rosin would have coped in my situation. It made me feel ashamed again because at least I still had my health. He had been disabled, and the odds were stacked so high against him, but he never felt sorry for himself or gave up on himself like I was doing right now. He never lost his positive spirit and he achieved so much with his life.

Or was my dream reminding me that my angels had not forgotten me? Mr Rosin had told me to remember who I was. I had, after all, been born into a family of psychics and spiritualists. Surely my belief in the world of spirit, even though I didn't think I had encountered it myself, should have been my comfort and my guide during this rough time.

Or, simplest of all, was my dream just reprimanding me for being so self-absorbed? I knew that I should not be crumbling under the pressure. I knew that there were many people in the world far worse off than me – people starving in the third world; people living in countries with corrupt governments; people born with birth defects or disabilities, like Mr Rosin – but however much I tried to remind myself that things could be far worse for me, it didn't seem to motivate me. I couldn't stop feeling sorry for myself. I couldn't step away from myself and my misfortunes. My perspective had shrunk so much. So, instead of inspiring me in the short term, the dream actually had the opposite effect. I felt more like a failure than ever before, and then things took an even greater turn for the worse. One morning, after working an early bird cleaning shift in a restaurant, I was walking back to the hostel when I heard footsteps behind me and felt a hand grab my arm.

I tried to get away but then I saw that my attacker was carrying a small knife. Immediately I handed over my bag and in a daze watched him run off with what little I had in the world. I just stood there in the street and cried as I have never cried before. I know people walked past, and they probably wondered what this girl was doing standing there sobbing, but nobody stopped. I don't blame them. They probably thought I was drunk or mad.

At that moment I wanted to die, or at the very least blot out any form of feeling, and in my mind I pictured myself going to several chemists and buying some sleeping pills. It was a very dark moment in my life.

Eventually I trudged back to my lodgings. Mercifully, my keys were in my pocket so at least I could get back inside. When I got in I noticed there was a letter for me on the table where the post was laid out. I knew who it was from. It was from an old college friend. I recognised her flowery handwriting immediately. We had kept in touch sporadically over the years but recently I had stopped replying to her letters because I felt such a loser and she was really doing well. She was engaged to be married and had just signed a fantastic five-book deal. I was single and doing a series of jobs I hated.

I opened the letter and noticed that it was an invitation to her book launch. The post must have been delayed because the invite was for this afternoon. Normally I would have thrown it in the bin, as I didn't need more salt rubbed in my wounds, but at that moment, for no reason at all, my dream flashed into my mind. I remembered Mr Rosin angrily telling me to not lose sight of my past. On a more material level, I also noticed on the invitation that there were refreshments on offer. My stomach was growling, and I had hardly any money to buy food, so I decided to go.

I found myself walking to the party. It took me a couple of hours and when I arrived the place was packed. The smell of the food was so tempting. As if in a trance, I headed straight for the buffet and ate and ate and then the worst thing happened: my old friend came up to me and gave me a warm hug. It felt a bit like that scene in the *Shirley Valentine* movie when the main character feels down and out and bumps into an old classmate who looks gorgeous. My friend looked amazing and I knew I looked terrible, but mercifully she was so taken up with her party that I don't think she really noticed. What she did do, though, before waltzing off to greet other guests, was introduce me to a friend of hers called Sam.

To cut a long story short, it turned out that Sam lived in the same area where I used to live with my mum before I went to university. He was a very chatty and animated man, and after discussing the weather, the buffet and how we knew my friend, we both went on to chat to other guests. I didn't think much of it until a week later when, out of the blue, I got a call from my friend. She told me that Sam had been in touch with her to say that he had been reading his local newspaper and had noticed in the ads section that a solicitor in the area was trying to locate someone of my name. She had even put a copy of the paper in the post so I could see for myself. It all sounded very odd – and I did wonder if it was someone else they were after – but curiosity got the better of my feelings of darkness and despondency, and the following day I called the number given.

When I called and explained who I was, the solicitor asked me a series of very unusual questions. I was asked about my work as a home help in the area, my home address when I used to live there, and what my interests were. My answers seemed to satisfy him because then he dropped his bombshell. For the past few years his firm had been trying to track me down; nobody had any address to contact me. The reason for the confusion was that when I left university my mum and dad had separated and I changed my surname out of loyalty to Mum as she had always been there for me, whereas my dad never had. My college friend still referred to me by my old name because I had never got round to telling her I had changed it, and this was the name by which she had introduced me to Sam. Mr Rosin would not have been aware of my name change and I had not been aware that he had left me a sum of money in his will – £10,000, to be exact.

I could not believe my ears when the solicitor told me the news. It was beyond astonishing. It was also incredibly moving because it showed just how much Mr Rosin really had believed in me. He knew that I had had a difficult start in life and he wanted to help me. I still get tears in my eyes to this day when I think about it. Even though the money came at a time when I really needed it, it wasn't only about the money; it was an even greater gift than that. From beyond the grave, Mr Rosin was telling me that he still believed in me; he felt I was worth something, even if I didn't.

Determined to make Mr Rosin proud, I used the money to buy a typewriter and get myself into more decent accommodation, and then I devoted myself to my dream of becoming a freelance writer. I had often talked to Mr Rosin about this dream and now in spirit he was giving me this opportunity to turn it into a reality. It wasn't easy – nothing worth achieving in life is – but slowly and surely I started to get a steady stream of work, which eventually led to my present career as a full-time writer.

So what exactly was it that saved me from a desperate situation and a downward spiral of despair? Was it the money? Was it my friend, or the actions of a helpful stranger? Was it my dream of Mr Rosin, or was it me?

It was probably a combination of all these things. I certainly needed the money, but I think what I needed more than anything else was an injection of self-belief and hope; just knowing that someone believed in me, cared about me, was truly life-changing. Without my old friend, or the actions of Sam, I might never have found out about the money, and I am deeply grateful to them both for their generosity of spirit, but deep down I think it may well have been my dream of Mr Rosin that was my real salvation.

Introduction: Saved by an Angel

I'd lost sight of my angels and dreaming of Mr Rosin a few days before finding out about his unexpected gift to me was just too much of a coincidence. Was it possible that he had reached out to me in spirit? Did he know that I would probably not have gone to that party without him encouraging me to remember my past? If I hadn't gone I might never have found out about the money left to me. For most of my life I had longed for reassurance from the world of spirit that this life doesn't end with death – and my longing intensified when my beloved mother died – but I never really felt that I got this solid reassurance. Although I believed in angels, because being born into a family of spiritualists this is what I had been brought up to believe, I still doubted whether they believed in me because I had never actually seen, heard or felt their presence for myself, but after that stunning dream of Mr Rosin it was hard for me to doubt that I had encountered an intersection between earth and heaven. It was hard for me not to believe that the world of spirit had visited me in my dreams. It was hard for me not to believe that this had been a supernatural experience.

Of course, all I am writing here is with the benefit of hindsight and it would take me many more years to truly believe that it wasn't all down to chance and that heaven was actually sending me a lifeline, but nonetheless from that moment on my confidence and self-belief grew and the veil between this world and the next gradually began to lift. I went on to have many more supernatural encounters, and as my life changed for the better I made it my mission to collect together in book form stories from people whose lives have also been saved or healed by angels. Some of these awesome stories you will find gathered together for you here in this book.

Something deeper

When lives are dramatically saved or healed or people encounter a stroke of incredible good fortune, you'll often hear the word 'miracle' being used. There is a strong belief that a higher power must have been at work. It's out of our hands. I'm not denying that such miracles can and do occur – and you'll certainly find breathtaking stories like this here – but what I want to point out is that there are many different kinds of miracles and the most transformative and enduring ones may, in fact, be the ones we don't pay enough attention to.

Let me explain. My psychic dream of Mr Rosin wasn't only the catalyst for the development of my psychic powers; it also led to something perhaps far more important – my spiritual growth. It helped me understand that it is not supernatural encounters that truly matter; what truly matters is what is going on inside you. If your heart is filled with love, kindness, peace and compassion, then something miraculous is already happening. My friendship with Mr Rosin taught me that.

You see, I do often wonder why Mr Rosin made the decision to leave me some money. When I befriended him I simply enjoyed his company and admired his optimism and determination. He was a role model, and spending time chatting to him a real delight. As for his severe disabilities and physical disfigurements, they were never a problem for me. When I was talking to him I saw only an incredible person with a brilliant mind who happened to be in a wheelchair. I guess I shall never really know the reason why Mr Rosin put me in his will, but I suspect it may have something to do with the fact that, without an agenda, I happily gave my time to talk to him and share my hopes and dreams of the future. It did not occur to me at the time, but in his winter years I may have been the only bright light in his life.

In other words, I spontaneously and unconditionally gave my time and energy to another person with no strings attached. My mum often used to tell me that as far as unconditional love and kindness is concerned there is always a ripple effect in the world of spirit. Lives are touched and changed as a result. Our reward rarely manifests in material things but in something far greater – spiritual wealth. At the time I thought this was a beautiful and lofty ideal, and I never would have believed that one day I would see this universal law, the ripple effect of kindness, in action; that one day I would be one of those rare and fortunate people who witness the results of their actions while they are still on this earth. I felt truly humbled. My angels were showing me the way forward. If more of my actions, thoughts and feelings were inspired by the same unconditional love, kindness and compassion I gave to Mr Rosin I would never feel spiritually impoverished again, however hard or tough my life got. I would never lose sight of my angels again.

This was the true life-saving message my angels were sending me. Unless I lived for love and was guided by my heart, I would never truly feel fulfilled. I needed to understand that the journey and the meaning of my life is not about what I achieve, but about how much I have loved. If the motivating force of my life was love, I would never feel alone, abandoned, worthless or afraid any more.

I thought my unhappiness was due to my dire financial situation, and the fact that my angels seemed to have deserted me, but I was wrong on both counts. You only need to look at the unhappy lives of many celebrities and fabulously rich people to know that money and material things can never bring true and lasting happiness. Sure, the money helped me, and came just at the right time, but it was not the true source of my salvation because, like all material things, it soon ran out, and I needed to find more again. What truly saved me was the beginning of an understanding that there had always been an aspiring angel within me waiting to energise and enrich my life with love and joy. I just hadn't been able to recognise or see it before because it was hidden by layers of self-doubt, guilt and fear. I had to stop looking around me for salvation, and look within first. There inside me was all the power, all the promise, all the love and all the spirit I needed.

So, the real magic wasn't really my psychic dream; the real magic was the spiritual awareness that experience brought me. Just as the room I had been living in had no view, my mind and my heart had shut down and it was my closed mind and heart that had limited me, not my difficult situation. My angels had been with me all along; I had just been looking for them in the wrong place.

During the many years I've been collecting real-life angel stories I've noticed that even though the stories are unique, they all have this similar theme of being saved from the inside out. This is even the case for stories of last-minute rescues from physical danger or spontaneous healing when salvation appears to come from an outside source. The encounter typically coincides with a heartfelt prayer, or becomes the catalyst for dramatic change in a person's life. Sometimes the trigger is direct angelic intervention, but more often than not the transformation, the spiritual awareness, starts from within, and that is when lives are truly saved and healed as a result.

Another common thread I've noticed is that each angel story in itself can also be a messenger of salvation, a trigger for deep spiritual growth. This is because whenever inspiring and life-affirming stories are shared they truly can save the lives of those who read or hear them, even if these people have not had an angel experience themselves, by reassuring them that the power of love and goodness is alive in this world and by reminding them that it is possible for anyone to catch a glimpse of heaven on earth.

Heaven on earth

I have always believed in heaven and for as long as I can remember I've been in love with the idea of angels. It's only in the last ten or so years, though, that I have really begun to understand that angels don't just exist in some lofty spiritual or astral realm that only mediums or psychics can access – they can manifest themselves to anyone with an open heart and mind at any time.

The key words here are 'an open mind'. An open mind can lead to new possibilities and with new possibilities comes the prospect of transformation. An open mind can lift the veil between this world and the next. Without an open mind a person's heart would never be able to recognise the presence of angels in their lives. So, as you read this book – whether you believe in angels or not – all you need to do is open your mind to the possibility that they may be real, and then let the stories weave their magic in your life as they did for the lives of the people you will read about.

It took me too many long years to realise that all I needed was an open mind and a trusting heart. Growing up in a spiritualist household I longed, yearned to see spirits and angels like my mother, grandmother and brother could. It was like bashing my head against a brick wall. The harder I tried, the further away they seemed to fly and the more alone, useless and disappointed I felt. I had no idea that my angels were with me, and within me, from the very start and that my obsession with whether or not I had the 'gift', along with a heavy dose of fear, were closing my eyes, heart and mind to them.

It's only really been in the last decade of my life – from my late thirties onwards – that I have begun to understand that while I couldn't see angels in the way mediums can, all along they were saving my life, offering me glimpses of the divine, through psychic dreams like the one I had of Mr Rosin or through unexpected feelings of love, warmth and joy, inspiring thoughts, stunning coincidences, gentle signs from the other side or through the selfless actions of strangers.

For example, when I was a little girl did an unseen hand lift my head above the water and save my life when I almost drowned? Years later when I was pregnant with my son and driving towards a junction did my mother in spirit call my name and urge me to turn right instead of left as I'd intended? If I had turned left I would almost certainly have died in a road accident. Was it the love of my angels that gave me the strength to pull through periods of depression and darkness in my life following the death of my mother and again when I had my children? Did an angel save my baby son from falling down a flight of stairs?

I could go on and on with other remarkable instances when I believe angels have saved me. And perhaps the most astonishing thing in all this is that I am no medium or angel lady – I am an ordinary forty-something mum of two with no remarkable psychic powers – but despite this lack of 'sight', miraculous things have happened to me, and continue to happen, that I can't explain. This has led me to believe that each one of us is born with the ability to catch a glimpse of heaven on earth, and that even though hardship, poverty, loss and layers of self-doubt, pessimism and fear can stop us believing we all have a lifeline, we can all find ways to cut through the layers. We can all look deep inside our hearts and rediscover our belief in angels and the spiritual healing or sense of wholeness that is our birthright, our meaning and our true salvation.

All of us at times in our lives, even those who seem to be blessed with every good fortune, cannot escape a feeling of 'is this it?' – an emptiness, a yearning for meaning, or something more than the everyday reality. Sometimes this feeling is like a longing to be rescued or transported to another time and place, a place where there is no fear and struggle, only magic and love. The rational part of our nature cannot see this place, but our hearts can sense that it has something to do with heaven or nirvana, or whatever name we give it. Deep inside each one of us our spirit longs to find a piece of this bliss on earth.

The wonderful news is that more and more ordinary people, like me and you, are catching their own glimpse of heaven on earth – and as this book will make clear, angels are saving people's lives and miracles are happening all the time. Sure, there are astonishing people who actually see angels or the spirits of those who have passed over, but as I never tire of pointing out, this is extremely unusual. It is far more usual to remember a fragment of a dream or to experience a profound flash of insight or inspiration. Also common are dazzling coincidences, meaningful signs, such as the appearance of a white feather at significant times, familiar scents or sounds or simple but incredibly comforting feelings of warmth and support during periods of loneliness, loss or trauma. And sometimes angels will manifest themselves through animals, or children, or through the spirits of departed loved ones consciously or unconsciously guided from a higher realm.

The possibilities for love and goodness to reveal themselves in this life, and offer tempting glimpses of the next, are without end but, to risk repeating myself, until we understand that the most powerful way to discover heaven is from within, because it is the angel inside us who can point the way to all other angels, we will never feel truly comforted and supported. In other words, experiencing supernatural encounters, or chasing after evidence of spirits, can't ever change or save your life. It isn't the answer. True joy springs from the angel within you and is not dependent on any external circumstances, person or condition. So, if you take anything away from this book I hope it will be to switch your focus away from uncovering so-called proof of angelic intervention and move it towards the aspiring angel that I know is within you.

You may wonder how I can be so sure that there is an aspiring angel within you and my answer is simple. I'm sure because you are holding this book in your hands. I don't know how you came across it – perhaps you bought it, were given it or found it lying around somewhere – but however you came to be reading it the angel within you guided you towards it. Incredible, really, when you think of the millions of other books out there that you could be reading. It's beyond coincidence. Believe me, you were *meant* to read it.

The angel inside you is guiding you every step of the way. It is guiding you right now as you read this and when you let heaven guide you in this way you can't go wrong; you discover a meaning and a fulfilment to your life that you have always been longing for. Whether you have encountered celestial beings or not, the fact that you are drawn to the idea of them is an expression of your essential goodness and divinity. You are already on the right path. Sure, it is not always possible to stay on the right path. All of us will have times when we stray into doubt and weakness or make the wrong choices, but that spark of essential goodness within us will never completely go out and if we can make the choice to follow it, however far we have strayed away, it will always save us. It will always guide us back towards the light.

Lighting up the world

And the more you welcome angels into your life, the more you light up the world for everyone else.

People all over the world today are awakening to the presence of angels, as I discovered first-hand when I started writing about angels. I began to receive countless letters and emails from people all firm in their belief that angelic intervention is not only possible but happens every day. These communications came from people of all backgrounds, faiths and cultures, proving that angels are truly non-denominational and are at long last emerging from religious strongholds and breaking through into the homes and hearts of ordinary people all over the world.

And the time has never been more right for angels to break through into our homes and hearts. Despite incredible technological, medical and material advances, our world remains full of pain, suffering and injustice. We are so used to the media screening terrible images of starving children, polluted landscapes and poverty-stricken communities that we are in danger of becoming desensitised. We urgently need to be reminded that there is still love and hope and compassion in the world and that the forces of goodness are more than a match for sadness, cruelty and pain. We urgently need to be reminded that each one of us, in our own unique way, can be a force for good. By dipping into the lives of ordinary people and showing them that they are stronger, more powerful and more magical than they ever thought they could be, our angels are reminding us that the goodness and justice we thought had been long forgotten still exists. They are guiding us to a new age, a new beginning. They are making themselves known to ordinary people – regardless of religion, background and culture – through astonishing but easily understood stories, because we have never needed to hear them as much as we do now.

The pages of this book

As you read the pages of this book prepare to be astonished, surprised, moved, and inspired – as I never fail to be – by the true stories of people whose bodies and spirits have been saved in some remarkable way by their guardian angel. In addition to the themes of deliverance, rescue, recovery or escape, another common narrative thread is that, to the best of my knowledge, all the stories you will read are true. In their own way they show just some of the visible and invisible ways in which angels reach out to us. Some of them will astonish you, some will puzzle you; some will move you and some may stretch your belief, but I have no reason to doubt the integrity of the people who gave me permission to share their experiences with you here. In some cases names and other details have been changed to protect identities, but I can assure you that in the great majority of cases the people who sent in their stories are ordinary people with ordinary lives, jobs and relationships. They are as real as real can be.

You'll read stories of dramatic and inexplicable rescues from danger or certain death, of well-timed coincidences or premonitions saving lives, coincidences that can only be explained by the existence of a higher power. There are also stories of angels working their magic through the spirits of loved ones, of angels simply bringing healing, comfort and warmth to those who feel that all hope is lost. Again, don't fall into the trap of thinking you need to be religious, psychic or a medium to see angels. Few of the people who submitted these stories would claim to have any special psychic or mediumistic powers. Some were religious, but others were not. Like more and more people these days they were spiritually inclined and believed in something, but they were not sure what. And last, but by no means least, there were those who believed in nothing at all until an angel stepped into their lives and changed everything. As always, it is a huge honour to share these deeply personal stories with a wider readership, and if you have been in touch with me to send me a story and don't find it here, forgive me, it is simply because time and space would not allow it, this time . . .

But just before I launch into these brilliant stories, in the first chapter of this book I'd like to share a little more of my own psychic journey with you. As in all my books I feel it is important for you to get a continuing sense of who I am, where I am coming from and why writing about angels is my passion. I hope my story will once again remind you that anyone – however unworthy or unqualified or sceptical, insecure and doubting of their psychic powers they may feel – can wake up one day and be saved by an angel.

CHAPTER ONE

My Redemption

Some people are so afraid to die that they never begin to live.

Henry Van Dyke

People living deeply have no fear of death.

Anaïs Nin

I will admit it. I'm scared of dying. I am very afraid. Sometimes I wake up in the middle of the night with an anxiety attack. This confession may surprise you, especially if you have read some of my previous books because you'll know that I believe wholeheartedly in an afterlife. I believe each one of us has a guardian angel who watches over us in this life and the next. I believe that angels can speak to us through our thoughts, feelings, hopes and dreams as well as through animals, other people and the spirits of loved ones who have passed to the other side. I believe they can also reveal themselves to us through coincidences and other gentle signs that have personal meaning to us.

Yes, I believe in an afterlife, but despite my powerful conviction, I have to confess that even though my fear of death does not dominate my thoughts all the time, I still get moments of tremendous panic and uncertainty. I'm still afraid of dying. I shouldn't be, but I am.

Indeed my whole life, as long as I can remember, I've been afraid of dying. The fear seems to hit me in waves, but it's always been there. Some of my earliest memories are dominated by this dread. One stands out in particular. I must have been about four, or barely five, and my mum was doing some household chores. I was sitting on the floor playing with my favourite doll and I just started weeping uncontrollably. For reasons I do not recall, I was convinced that my doll had died, so that afternoon when I was out in the garden I staged a burial. It was a very solemn affair indeed, but just before bedtime I couldn't bear the thought of my doll being alone and cold in the garden so I dug her up. I resurrected her. She looked a little worse for wear but we were reunited. Believing I had conquered death, I had a moment of fragile triumph.

That feeling of triumph didn't last long as months later my beloved grandmother died, followed soon after by my great-aunt. Try as I might to deny it, death was an inescapable reality for me now. My grandmother and great-aunt had both been such loving, larger-than-life characters and my childish mind could not make sense of the fact that they were gone for ever. I wouldn't be able to touch or talk to them any more. I went to both their funerals and found the experience utterly terrifying. One was a cremation and the other was a burial and both scared

2

the life out of me, giving me nightmares for a considerable amount of time afterwards. For some reason, the swish of the curtain as the coffin disappeared during the cremation freaked me out the most. To this day I still get moments of apprehension when I close the curtains at night, so I try to keep them open for as long as I can. If I had my way we wouldn't have any curtains in our house at all. It's the same when I go to the theatre. However brilliant the show, it's spoiled by the curtains closing at the end.

On another memorable occasion, a few years later, I was sitting beside Mum on a bus. I think I was about ten and we were on our way to a friend's birthday party. I should have been in high spirits with the prospect of games, balloons and cake, but again, for no reason I can recall, the feeling of dread washed over me. This time I was convinced that my mum was going to die. I cried so much, and rubbed my eyes so hard, that when we arrived at the party everyone thought I'd had an allergic reaction to something.

Things didn't ease when I got older. At junior school I'd be perfectly fine but then a morbid thought would flash into my head and I would be in pieces. In secondary school the fear reached fever pitch. I would think about death a lot of the time. If I had a headache I was convinced I had a brain tumour. If I was travelling in a car or train I would be anxious the whole time. At the end of the day I would constantly tell friends and family, 'Goodbye and I love you,' in case I never got to see them again, because my fears were strongest just before I went to sleep.

I guess it didn't help matters when, in my late teens, I got a weekend job at an old people's home. Death was all around me. It was heartbreaking every time a resident passed over. One day I would be bringing a meal to a resident and having a chat with them, or helping them complete a puzzle, and then the next day that resident wasn't alive any more. I shall never forget the first time I saw a dead body. It didn't look or feel real. It looked like a waxwork of the person I had known – there were similarities, but the essence of that person was no longer there.

By the time I went to college a good deal of my waking thoughts were preoccupied with death. It was dangerously close to controlling my life and my relationships. The thought of not feeling, not breathing, not thinking and my body being burned or buried underground made me sick to my stomach, literally. My terror was stopping me from experiencing life to the full. I'd avoid people or situations that I thought might put me in danger. My anxieties were preventing me from doing things I wanted to do, and being the person I wanted to be.

Things eased somewhat in my early twenties. I guess I was just too overwhelmed by the need to pay the bills to reflect on my mortality as much as before. And then in my mid-twenties came the defining moment of my life when my beloved mum died. Losing the person I loved most in the world was my worst nightmare. I felt alone and afraid as never before. I wanted to believe in an afterlife; I was sure I believed in an afterlife, but how could I be certain?

Regrettably, any belief I had in the afterlife didn't comfort me. Indeed, that belief was tested as never before when I didn't appear to receive any sign from my mum in spirit to reassure me. How I longed to glimpse her, hear her whisper in my ear, but however hard I longed and prayed for contact with the other side, all I got was silence. Sometimes I would find myself suddenly tearing through her things in search of a photo of her. I was petrified I might forget what she looked like. I needed to reassure myself that she had once been real.

Perhaps the most heartbreaking thing of all was her last diary. Mum was always organised, and never went anywhere without her diary. She died in November but in the diary were dates for appointments, meetings and so on in the December following. I wondered if when she was writing down these appointments she had known deep down she would not get to any of them. If she knew that, by then, her heart would have stopped beating and she would no longer be breathing.

The early years after my mother's death were the most lonely and uncertain of my life. I prayed for some sign from her from the world of spirit but however hard I prayed nothing seemed to come through. My mum seemed so very far away. I tried to learn all I could about the world of spirit, but it seemed that knowledge didn't comfort me. Forced to contemplate my own impermanence, there were many low times when I did wonder if this life was all there is.

My angels must have been watching over me though, because I did somehow manage to struggle through the endless, torturous months and years following my mother's death. The pain and hurt never left me, but the survival instinct kicked in and the pieces of my life did slowly start to come together as I went about forging a career, falling in love and getting married. And even though I never felt I received a clear and dramatic sign from my mum in spirit, I did gradually start to catch glimpses of her presence in dreams and through coincidences. It wasn't much, and it certainly wasn't earth-shattering, but it was enough to sustain and gently encourage me.

But things spiralled out of control again when I fell pregnant with my son, and two years later my daughter. I didn't relish my pregnancies at all as I was convinced each time I would die in labour. Then when my kids were born I was consumed by fears of dying too young and leaving them behind when they still needed me. I was scared of what would happen to them if I wasn't around to look out for them.

Over time, my fears of dying continued to haunt me. Sometimes I would feel absolutely fine – happy even – and they would appear out of the blue. I would be in the middle of some-thing and panic would inexplicably set in – I wouldn't be able to breathe, or my limbs would go tingly and numb, or my heart would start to race. It would feel like I was racing a marathon even if I hadn't moved. Then I would always feel completely exhausted afterwards, as if I really had run that marathon! Once, this feeling of dread consumed me when I was on a Tube train and there was a ten-minute delay between stations. I almost blacked out with fear.

And when I hit 'the big four-oh' my fear of dying started to get tangled up with my fear of ageing. Sometimes I would look in the mirror and not be able to recognise the reflection staring back at me. I would see lines, wrinkles and a mature woman looking back, the visible signs of ageing making it clear to me that my life on earth was finite and my days were numbered.

Even more unsettling was my paranoid fear of something happening to those I love, in particular my children. Every school trip or party with one of their friends was a source of huge anxiety to me. It was the same with my husband. He is several years older than me and I was forever anxious for his health, the thought of life without him too horrible to contemplate.

I'm guessing that everything I have said so far is still puzzling you considerably, especially as I've made it clear that I have an unshakeable belief in the afterlife. I've also clearly stated that this belief is based on some incredible, life-changing paranormal experiences I have had, as well as the thousands of personal testimonies I have read in the many years I have been researching and writing about the world of spirit.

Surely, you must be thinking to yourself, such a strong belief in the world of spirit would remove all fear of dying? I agree with you completely here. It is completely illogical. Why, after all the proof of the afterlife that I have gathered, and why after all the extraordinary experiences I have had, was I still waking up in the middle of the night with panic attacks? Surely as an angel author I should be able to sleep well at night, reassured and comforted by my absolute conviction in the world of spirit?

I don't blame you for asking this question. It's one I have asked myself countless times over the years, but it was only recently that I finally got the answer that I have unconsciously been seeking all my life. The comfort and sense of peace that answer brought me was beyond words and went on to inspire me to write this book in the hope that what you read will bring you a similar comfort. There have been many times in my life when I feel I have been rescued by my angels, but this time I was well and truly saved, liberated and redeemed. Here's what happened.

The gift

It was early in 2008 and I had had a good couple of years. My angel writing was going from strength to strength with titles serialised in national newspapers and hitting the *Sunday Times* bestsellers top ten. I was also making huge progress in my psychic development. On top of all that, my children were thriving at school and my husband was healthy and happy. After so many years of loss and hardship I was happier and more fulfilled than I had ever been. I was in a good place and incredibly grateful for that.

And then one Monday night I went to bed as normal. I remember feeling very content before I drifted off to sleep as it had been another really good day. Then for no apparent reason I woke with a start at about one in the morning. I don't know why I woke up. There wasn't some worrying issue on my mind. My husband wasn't snoring. There was no noise coming from outside and I hadn't had any distressing dreams. And yet there I was in the middle of the night shaking with fear. It had been a while – a good few years, in fact – since I had felt this level of apprehension. It was disappointing to find myself reacquainted with my familiar uncertainties about dying. I didn't like it at all.

For no reason I could understand, I felt, wave after wave of tremendous fear. I could hear my heart pounding so loudly I thought it would come out of my chest and I was struggling to breathe. I thought I was going to die and an unknown terrible thing was going to happen to me. I felt as though I had awakened from a dream to a cold reality and there was no possibility of return. My home, my children, my work, my favourite places would all evaporate with my death. Nothing was stable or enduring and what possible meaning could such a transient existence contain?

I became intensely aware of meaninglessness and nothingness. In that instant I lost sight of everything I thought I trusted and hoped for and could only think of oblivion. Pains were shooting down my chest and my legs. I was so afraid of dying that I couldn't catch my breath. What was happening to me? Was I having a heart attack? Was it for real this time? Was I actually dying? There was so much more I wanted to do. I wasn't ready.

Paralysed with foreboding and raw fear of dying at any second, I could do nothing but sit on my bed shivering and shaking. And then, as abruptly as it had arrived, the crushing feeling was gone, leaving behind a residue of uneasiness: when might the panic come again?

I tried to go back to sleep but it was impossible. The episode had left me deeply scared and wide awake. I knew I had to do something about it and resolved to visit my doctor in the morning. I had to find a way to deal with my fear. Eventually I got up to go downstairs and make myself a cup of tea. Still shaky and shivering, I remember clasping the handrails very tightly. I was worried I might fall and break my neck.

When I got downstairs I noticed that the kitchen light was on. It surprised me because I was usually very careful to switch off all the lights at night, and I had definitely been the last person to go upstairs. I grabbed the kettle and filled it with water and then I sat down and waited for it to boil. While I was sitting there I closed my eyes and prayed for my guardian angel to help me overcome my fears.

Soon the kettle started to boil and I set about making my cup of tea. I opened the kitchen cupboard to grab a tea bag and as I did, something fell out onto the floor with a clatter. I picked it up and saw that it was a DVD of *The Shawshank Redemption*. I had no idea how it got there because to the best of my knowledge we didn't own a copy and even if we did, why would anyone place it in the kitchen cupboard of all places?

Intrigued, I decided I might as well go into the living room and watch it. It had been many years since I had last seen it and I remembered it being a great movie. I headed out of the kitchen but when I tried to switch off the light the strangest thing happened: I flipped the switch but the light stayed on. I tried again and this time it did go off. It did strike me as odd but I can't say I read anything into it at the time.

I went to the living room and put the movie into the DVD player. I could feel myself yawning as the movie sprang alive and soon found myself fighting to stay awake despite the absorbing story. My eyelids got very heavy and I must have fallen asleep because the next thing I remember is waking up abruptly with one of the characters uttering the phrase, 'Get busy living or get busy dying.'

Suddenly, I was wide awake again. The words echoed in my head as I watched the movie until the end. They continued to whisper to me as I went back to bed and finally fell into a deep sleep. They were the first thing on my mind when I woke up the next morning and as I went about my routine the following day. They kept repeating themselves over and over again like a song you can't get out of your head.

Now you would have thought that I'd written enough angel books by now to recognise immediately that my guardian angel was speaking to me through my thoughts, the light in the kitchen and the words I had heard from the movie, but for some reason it took a while for this truth to sink in. I guess my guardian angel was coming up against years and years of uncertainty. My fears and anxieties about dying had become almost second nature and so even when comfort and hope were being offered to me, I didn't instantly recognise it. My guardian angel was persistent though, and those words, 'Get busy living or get busy dying,' just wouldn't leave me.

A few days later the truth at long last found a home in my heart. I was in my office working and my eyes felt sore and my head hurt a little, so I decided to take a break and look out of the window. It was a dreary, damp and cold morning and I found myself longing for some sunshine, for the first signs of spring. As I've done many times in my life I was wishing time away. I was thinking about some time in the future when things would be better than they are now, when I would feel happier than I did now. Yet again the phrase, 'Get busy living or get busy dying,' whispered through my mind and as it did I had one of those glorious 'ah-ha' moments of stunning, blinding, absolute clarity.

I realised then that all my life I had been constantly looking ahead to the future for an ultimate feeling of aliveness or happiness – when I was a child I thought that contentment would come when I grew up; when I grew up I thought it would come when I could see angels; when I started to catch glimpses of the other side it would be when I got married; when I got married it would be when I became a mother. I think you get the picture. All my life I had been constantly looking ahead of myself to a time and place when everything in my life would be OK. In the process, I wasn't fully engaging with the present moment and it was for this reason that death held such fear for me. I was afraid of dying before the future I had always been anticipating – the future when I thought I would feel really alive – had happened.

So it wasn't death I was really afraid of – what scared me was not living my life to the full, but as far as that was concerned there was something I could do about it. The reality was that whatever fulfilment I was searching for was and always had been waiting for me to discover it in this very moment, in the here and now. If I could stop focusing on what will be, and live every moment of my life for its own sake instead, I would no longer be postponing life or happiness. I would be experiencing life and happiness by using each moment completely and fully, no matter how mundane. In this way I would be constantly fulfilled; constantly alive in the present.

When each moment is lived fully and completely, there isn't room to fear death. Sacrificing the present moment for a future that does not exist yet had been the root cause of my fears and anxieties. In reality, life is just one continuous, present moment; the future was only a notion in my mind. I had a choice: I could spend my life alive in the present or dead in the future. I could get busy living or I could get busy dying! From that day on I made the decision and the commitment to choose life, and from that moment on I can honestly say I have uncovered the secret of eternal life. Death has lost its sting for me.

It would be a lie to say that I don't get any anxieties and fears about dying any more. I still have many fears but I don't wrestle with them as I used to. Indeed, I hope I will always experience them because it is only deep faith that can admit fear and then move on to understand that angels can work through our doubts as well as our certainties. Instead of beating myself up when I feel scared, I think of these anxious feelings as a gift from the world of spirit – a gift to remind me to seize the day, choose eternal life in every moment; in short, to wake up and live my life to the full.

It took me close to forty-five years to understand the simple, profound, life-saving truth – and my understanding is still evolving – that eternal life isn't something we will experience after death, but something we can experience now, in the present. It took me a lot of heartache and pain to understand that however much proof you collect of an afterlife – either by reading stories of spirits and near-death experiences or even by experiencing something paranormal yourself – it won't give you the sense of meaning, comfort and certainty you crave. The only way to get a handle on your fears and live life to the full is to savour every precious moment of your life, starting right here, right now.

Right here, right now

Think about it. The present moment is all we really have while we are on this earth. It is a wonderful gift to us from our angels, because it offers us an endless flow of opportunities to grow spiritually. It is the doorway to the invisible realm.

While I was writing this chapter, I wondered many times how many people there must be out there like me who have found it hard to live in the present moment, or wondered if there is any meaning or purpose to their lives, or if there is a guardian angel watching over them. I want to ask all those people to pause for a moment and ask themselves if they are OK in the present moment. If you don't think you are OK, ask yourself if you are still breathing – if so, then you are OK.

Believe it or not, you really do have the power within you to create peace in any moment. You don't have to wait any more. If you still feel lost, then ask the angels inside you for help. Ask your angels to bring you light, love and peace.

You are never alone if you believe in angels. If you believe that everything in your life, however tough, happens for a reason and if you seek to learn the lesson or find the blessing, you are on the right path. Use your breathing as a guide; it is your spirit and it can always guide you back to the present moment where the gift of peace can be found.

Remember too that your angels are unlikely to appear to you in the traditional manner. The present moment may bring many wonderful secrets and gifts. Perhaps a hunch or an insight changes your mind and your life for the better? Perhaps a coincidence will transform everything? Perhaps the kind words of a stranger or a loved one will help you through a difficult time? Perhaps the loving companionship of a pet can bring you joy when you need it the most? Perhaps you will be inspired by the beauty of a sunrise or sunset? Perhaps the lyrics of a song you happen to hear speak to your heart? Perhaps you will see an angel in the most unlikely places or sense the divine in the most unexpected ways.

And perhaps if you are still convinced that there is no magic for you in the present moment, reading the stories in the next few chapters will be the turning point. Perhaps they will help you become aware of the subtle ways angels can weave their wonder and magic in your life. Perhaps it will help you see that every moment of every day you are indeed entertaining angels unawares, and with every breath you take there is an eternal divine spark within.

Ever since my first angel book, *An Angel Called My Name*, was published in 2008 I have often referenced the British romantic poet William Blake, a man who saw and heard angels all his life. Blake once famously wrote that he could see the world in a grain of sand, so why not see it in a blade of glass, a butterfly, a dew drop, a sunrise, a starry night, the comfort of a coincidence, or anything that amazes and inspires you? Why not hear angels calling your name in the sound of birdsong or in the whispers of departed loved ones in your dreams or in your heart? And why not let this book work a life-saving miracle inside you and inspire you to see the world for what it truly is: a place of surprising wonder?

Angel stories are lasting reminders that love and goodness are real and powerful and ever-present forces in our lives. They are reassuring messages that the magical journey of this life does not end with death. They are also evidence that even though we can't always see, hear or touch it, our world is connected to the world of spirit and all we need to do to connect with it and discover eternal life is to open our minds to its divine presence in our lives and in our hearts.

And remember, there is never any better time to establish, or reinforce, our connection to the divine than the present moment. There is no better time than right now to be reminded of something we once knew, but tend to forget along the way: angels watch over and protect us and death is not an end but a beginning.

> *'End? No, the journey doesn't end here. Death is just another path, one that we all must take. The grey rain curtain of this world rolls back, and all turns to silver glass, and then you see it.'*
> *Gandalf,* The Lord of the Rings

Waking up

At some point in life – sometimes in our teenage years, some-times later – each of us will find that death moves to the forefront of our thoughts. For some of us this may happen rarely, but for others, as was the case for me, it can happen regularly and with great intensity. There are so many triggers. Perhaps you are watching a news report about a natural disaster where countless innocent lives are snuffed out, or perhaps you read about a murder in the newspapers. Perhaps the death of a loved one or someone you know brings you face to face with your mortality. Perhaps you drive past a terrible accident on the motorway on your way home from work.

Or perhaps a glance in the mirror at a cluster of fresh wrinkles; greying hair; a milestone birthday; meeting a friend you haven't seen for ages and being shocked at how he or she has aged; seeing old photos of yourself; the diagnosis of someone we know with a serious disease, like cancer – or perhaps there is no trigger at all, just a sudden feeling of dread, uncertainly and fear. In an instant, death or dying are not something abstract or distant, or something that happens to other people, but something we have no choice about confronting.

What do you feel when you have such experiences? What do you do? Do you try to distract yourself from your thoughts with work, everyday routines and frantic activity? Do you go for botox or cosmetic surgery to try and turn back the clock?

I implore you not to try to distract yourself or ignore how you feel, because in the depths of your despair you are being offered an opportunity for great spiritual growth. Instead, let the feeling linger with you as you think about the advantages of remaining aware that death comes to us all. This awareness can encourage you to enhance your life while you are still in this body. It can help you see that without darkness there would be no light. It can help you feel greater compassion and love for yourself and others.

It can help you understand that not only are love and compassion forces for good, they are also your essence, what truly defines you.

And by awakening in this way to the bittersweetness of your mortality you will become acutely aware that whenever there is compassion and love inside your heart, or manifesting in the world around you, there is also a doorway to heaven and a stairway to eternity. You will know that you are stronger than death. And it is my dearest wish that this book, and every angel encounter story you read in it, will reassure and remind you of this life-changing and life-saving truth.

Angelic encounters

But before you move on, what exactly is an angel encounter?

All encounters with angels are stories of life-saving divine rescue, courage, generosity, selflessness, blessings, compassion, encouragement and magic in everyday life, as well as just-in-the-nick-of-time aid by guardians, both real and in spirit, who ensure a person's safety through periods of danger or darkness.

An angel encounter is a manifestation of heaven on earth, a moment in a person's life when they meet their eternal celestial guide and inspiration. As discussed in the introduction, this meeting is more likely to occur if your mind is open to the idea, but it can also happen without any expectation at all. And the form it takes may be anything at all. There is no right or wrong as far as our angels our concerned. Anything or anyone that can awaken forgotten hopes and unsung dreams and inspire us to become more than we believe we can be is an angel encounter.

All those who believe in angels have their own stories to share, stories that can nourish the hearts and spirits of all those who read or hear them. Sadly, many of the people who got in touch with me while I was writing this book told me that this was the first time they had shared their magnificent narratives. They had wanted to talk about their experiences before but were concerned that they might be judged or that people would not believe them, so incredible were their stories in some cases. Many told me it was a relief to be able to share them now with other like-minded souls.

The purpose of sharing these deeply personal stories from ordinary people is to show that even though we often define ourselves by our differences, be those differences of religion, wealth, status, culture and so on, when it comes to angel encounters we all share a common bond with the divine. Heaven is a force that unites and calls us all and an angel story is a messenger from heaven.

So don't be surprised if you feel a surge of energy, a sort of spiritual electric shock, when you read or talk about angelic encounters. When I first started gathering and writing up angel stories, and sharing some of my own in book form, it was a moment of profound revelation. I realised that angels have always been with me, even if I didn't understand or notice them at the time, and this realisation was the miracle, the surprise of my life I had been longing for. The word angel lit me up from the inside, energised me, because I knew that the words I was writing and recording were for everyone. It became clear that when magical experiences are shared, read or heard they confirm the existence of angels and by so doing they help answer questions we thought we might never find the answers to. They help us find true spiritual guidance by forcing us to look within ourselves for answers and comfort.

They can help us become happier people – all we need to do is let them.

Calling all angels

And just before you read on, I'd like you to reflect a moment on your life and all those times when you thought hope was lost but perhaps there was something or someone that gave you meaning, strength or purpose again. Perhaps it was a chance meeting, a stroke of good fortune or the helpful words of a loved one or the loving actions of friends or a pet. Or perhaps that something came from deep inside you in a dream, a hunch or insight or unexpected feelings of warmth that inexplicably made you feel better about yourself and gave you the strength to move forward again. Hindsight is a fabulous teacher. Reconnect with these magical and intense memories because they can help you rediscover the angel inside you and when you do that your life will never be the same again. You will begin to see the footprints of angels in your life and all around you.

As you search through your memories, remember that messages from heaven will reveal themselves in the most unexpected and unlikely ways. In looking back at my life I have found that I was saved by many different things. At the time they may not have seemed like the work of my angels, but now I can clearly see that they were. Spontaneous feelings of connectedness to a loved one in spirit, flashes of intuition, coincidences, angel signs and dreams are all common ways for heaven to talk to us, but there are countless other methods by which angels can save your life because they prefer to reveal themselves in ways that have deep, personal meaning to each individual. And if you aren't sure whether celestial beings have saved your life, listen to your heart. It always knows the answer because it is in your heart that your angels first make their home.

If you feel that you can't remember anything miraculous in your life, or that you have never seen or felt your angels, then be prepared for everything in your life to change from this moment on, because reading this book can be your turning point: the moment in your life when you finally became aware of the subtle ways angels reveal themselves to you; the moment when you see clearly that within you there has always been and always will be a piece of heaven. I want the stories that you read here to offer you understanding, hope, encouragement and love. I want them to remind you that you can be stronger than you ever thought possible and that your life can be more magical than you ever dreamed. I want them to show you that death is nothing to fear and that in spirit you will never end. Through these pages I want to encourage you to take the first step forward into the rest of your eternal life.

And whether you recall or recognise for first time the presence of the divine in your life, I urge you to share your story with me and become a messenger from heaven yourself (details about how to do so can be found on page 251 of this book). As I say in all my books, the more people talk about angels and share their inspiring stories with each other the easier it is for angels to light up the world. They are always close by and the more you acknowledge their presence, the more you remember and notice them, the more likely you are to see and feel them. Remember, you don't need any special prayer or invocation, and you certainly don't need to belong to any religion or to have so-called mediumistic or psychic powers to see angels. Just cultivate an attitude of gratitude and respect, let go of notions of what an angel should or should not be, and keep your eyes and your heart open. This is because the more you see love, goodness and beauty all around you, the more you expect the unexpected, the more heavenly and magical your life will become.

Divine moments are in front of us all. So stop waiting for something or someone to save you, and save yourself instead by opening your heart and letting your angels in, right here and right now.

This is and always will be your moment. Why not grab hold of it?

I held a moment in my hand, brilliant as a star, fragile as a flower,
a tiny sliver of one hour. I dripped it carelessly, Ah! I didn't know,
I held opportunity.

Hazel Lee

CHAPTER TWO

Heavenly Rescues

What we do not see, what most of us never suspect of existing, is the silent but irresistible power which comes to the rescue of those who fight on in the face of discouragement.

Napoleon Hill

This is a miracle from God.

Alberto Avalos, uncle of the first Chilean miner to be rescued

So far, I've talked about some of the subtler, gentler ways that angels can dip into our lives, but the stories you'll read in this chapter may well sink deeper into your heart. These stories aren't about coincidences, twists of fate or sudden profound realisations that transform everything. As awesome and inspiring as such stories are, they may not have the same impact as the stories that follow. That's because you are now going to read about life-or-death situations.

It's amazing when gentle signs from the world of spirit reach out to you, but when your life – or the life of someone you care about – is saved from injury or certain death, the impact can be awe-inspiring and tremendous. The narratives here cannot be dismissed as chance or coincidence, because it is overwhelmingly clear that unexplainable and truly remarkable events occurred to rescue these people from or prevent a situation that could well have killed them.

In almost all cases the people involved told me that the heavenly intervention was unprompted. They were typically not aware that they were in danger and during the crisis there was often no time to hope or pray for divine protection. They did not know what lay ahead but their guardian angel clearly did know and either sent them an emphatic warning through unexpected and powerful thoughts or feelings, or intervened more directly and drastically.

For those who believe in angels, no explanation is necessary. For others, possible answers can be found from a quantum scientific perspective, which argues that everything and everyone is interlinked, that time is a delusion and that the only reality is what a person sees or feels. But no matter the explanation that may be put forward there is no escaping the fact that in all these next stories 'something' either truly miraculous or simply inexplicable intervened to prevent a tragedy occurring. I believe that this 'something' was a higher power and that is why it seems impossible not to be inspired and astonished when reading these true accounts of people whose lives have been well and truly touched – and saved – by angels.

I'm going to start with this dramatic story sent to me by Charlotte.

Flying through the air

Fifteen years ago, when I was twelve, I had this incredible experience. I was at that vulnerable age when what my friends thought about me was all that really mattered. Anyway, I was walking to school with my mum. She still liked to walk with me even though I really didn't want her to. She told me that she would stop when I was thirteen, and I couldn't wait to become a teenager. It just wasn't cool, me hanging around with Mum.

On that particular day we were about to cross the busy road just outside the school entrance and I felt my mum grab my hand as she usually did. My friends were waiting for me on the other side and I felt too embarrassed to hold her hand. So I tore my hand angrily away from hers and started to cross the street on my own. Within a heartbeat this car was about to hit me but instead of it crashing into me I felt myself being lifted up in the air by a pair of huge, strong arms and then gently placed down again. I remember hearing my mum scream and seeing my waiting friends look shocked. I remember my mum running over to me and the driver stepping out of his car, but I didn't feel a thing. It was as if I was watching the scene unfold from somewhere else. Everything took place in slow motion. There wasn't a scratch on me. Everyone was crying, but I just lay there feeling elated.

I believe that my guardian angel saved me that day. I can't think of any other explanation. I just hope my story inspires others out there who don't believe in angels because I think it proves they are real; without them I would not be writing to you today. My eyes feel wet with tears as I write this to you and every time I think back to that day my heart fills with feelings of love.

25

I don't know why my life was spared. I went on to get OK qualifications at school and a decent job and am happily married now, but I don't think I have done anything special with my life yet. I mean, I haven't found a cure for cancer and I haven't raised millions of pounds for charity. I'm just an ordinary woman with an ordinary life, but my experience taught me that we are all special to our angels. We can all be extraordinary in our own way.

Charlotte's story is astonishing and I wanted to place it first because she raises an issue that I know is a source of continuing confusion and frustration to many people: why are some people seemingly saved or protected by the angels when others are not?

We may never know the answer to this common question until we pass over to the other side and can see the bigger picture of our lives. As humans we live in linear time, but our angels live in spiritual time, so we may never understand why bad things happen to good people until we also live in spiritual time. It's possible that the answer is just too complex for the human mind to handle, or perhaps when a person experiences suffering in this life it is part of their soul's spiritual journey. Sometimes the most important lessons are learned through hardship and struggle, the seed of light is born in the darkest hour. Our angels may weep with and for us, but maybe sometimes they know that they cannot intervene, or make choices for us, because they cannot interfere with our free will and must allow our spirits the freedom to grow.

I've used the words perhaps and possibly a lot here and, to be honest with you, I really don't know why some people escape danger or survive illness whereas others are not so fortunate or die far too young. All I can do is give you my personal thoughts and I've always favoured the 'it's not your time' theory. I also believe that the best thing we can ever do is live our lives in a manner that our guardian angel approves of, so when hardship strikes or darkness descends we can find comfort in the thought that we are not alone. And then when the time comes for us to pass over to the other side not only can we take our guardian angel's hand and fly without fear, guilt and regret to our new spiritual home, we will know that the world we leave behind us is a better place because we were once a part of it.

To return to the miracles that saved lives as the theme of this chapter, I'm going to follow on now with this enlightening story sent to me by Rachel.

All the way

When I was ten years old I was abused by a family member and when I told my mum and dad, they did not believe me. I was torn. My family could not cope with my self-harming and took me to see a specialist, but nothing helped me.

When I turned eighteen I had lost contact with my mum and dad because they couldn't cope with my mental illness so I went to live with a support worker and was given 24/7 care. I didn't hear from my family for two years. Then, at the age of twenty-one, I tried to jump off a car park building. I didn't, though, because when I tried to jump I felt something or someone tap me on the shoulder. I heard a voice tell me that even though my family seemed to have abandoned me they still loved me in their hearts. I turned around to see who was talking to me but there was no one there. As I looked around I knew in my heart that the voice I had heard was right and my family did still love me.

An angel saved my life and I am now in a secure unit taking my meds and slowly getting better. Since that day in the car park I have started to see that my life is worth living. Every time I feel down I hear that voice telling me that I am loved and it stops me from feeling alone or trying to harm myself in some way. My angel is always there for me, all the way.

I wrote back to Rachel to thank her for sharing her story, as clearly her life so far has been a tough journey, but I also told her that now her heart has begun to open to the love of her angels she is entering a new and wonderful phase, where nothing will ever feel the same again.

Nothing has ever felt the same for Carol either after an angel saved her life when she was a young mother in her early twenties.

On impulse

I was walking home from a trip to the town where I lived, pushing my son along in the pushchair – he was about two at the time. Every time we took this trip (which was quite regularly) I always walked the same route. We walked across the park, through a short alleyway between some houses at the edge of an estate and would usually continue walking straight along the road. I did not usually veer from this route as it would have meant crossing the road on a corner.

On this particular day I reached the corner and suddenly had the thought that I should cross the road. Even though it was on a corner and there was a car coming, I had such a strong impulse to cross the road that I just did it without thinking.

The car came down the road towards us, took the corner too fast and then went up the pavement at exactly the point where I would have been walking with my son in the pushchair if I had not crossed the road. If I had taken my usual route and not listened to the warning in my head, then we would surely have been knocked over and either seriously injured or killed.

Joanne also believes an angel is saving her life every day.

Off white

I have had a very stressful and difficult two years. I am thirty-nine years old and the mother of five children. Two years ago I started to have flashbacks and ultimately remembered childhood sexual abuse. This was a really distressing time for me and I don't know how I coped.

The date I remembered the abuse was 21 August 2008 and exactly one year after that date my youngest daughter was born. It feels as if she was sent to me to enable me to cope and carry on with my life. I underwent counselling and it's been like a rollercoaster ride. In October 2010 I felt so low and unable to carry on with the knowledge of what had happened to me that when I went to bed I looked at my husband's belt lying there and contemplated hanging myself. I got into bed and I know that I wasn't properly asleep. At first I felt that someone was dragging me towards the window but I didn't want to go and then out of nowhere lots and lots of large, thick angel wings covered my entire body as if they were soothing me. They were an off white colour and huge with no body attached, just large wings. I woke up and felt different, calmer.

From that moment I knew that I couldn't go any lower than I had that night and I changed my thought pattern. I had to carry on for my children and I deserved to live. It's only been a few months but I am a lot stronger now and I know angels are protecting and watching me. I'm not scared of what's on the other side as I know death isn't the end. This experience seemed surreal but reading your book has made me realise that I did have an angel experience that night.

I've had a number of heartbreaking stories like this sent to me by victims of abuse and what is awe-inspiring about them is that, even though they might be considered the very last people on earth to believe in angels, many of them are drawn towards a strong belief in the angels' loving power.

I'd like to share Sally's story with you now.

At the window

When I was nineteen, I went to a club and ended up flirting with a guy I met. He seemed really cool and I'm not denying that I fancied him. After a few hours talking and drinking we decided to leave the club together. I had had quite a bit to drink but I was certainly not drunk. This guy offered to drive me home. In the back of my mind I did think that he might be expecting more from me, but I didn't think he was the kind of guy to try anything on. As I said, he seemed like a really cool guy, straight-talking and decent. How wrong I was.

When we got to the street where I live I pointed out where my house was but instead of parking outside my front door, he parked several houses away. He leaned over to kiss me, but I made it clear I wasn't ready for that. He got angry and I heard the car doors shut. I told him to back off but he wouldn't leave me alone. I started to get very frightened. It was late and the street was dead quiet. There was no one around for me to bang on the windows to cry for help. This guy was going to rape me. And nobody would believe me if I said I had been raped as we had been flirting outrageously in the club. I had been so stupid getting into the car of a man I hardly knew. I can't say I prayed but I did think about my mum and longed to be home with her. She was probably fast asleep by now and completely unaware of the horror I was going through. And then at that very same moment my mum's face appeared at the car window. The guy got the shock of his life and let go of me, giving me time to unlock the car doors and get out. Cursing, he sped away as fast as he could. I turned around to hug Mum but she wasn't there. I was alone on the street.

I ran home as fast as I could and burst into Mum's bedroom. She was fast asleep so I shook her awake and told her everything that had happened. My mum cried tears of relief and told me that she had been thinking a lot about me but she hadn't felt worried or anything. She was used to me staying out late and thought I was a sensible girl so she had no cause to worry. She was furious with me for being so stupid as to get into that guy's car and I know I will never do anything like that again. I've learned my lesson.

What I'd like to ask you, though, is what happened? I promise you that both that monster of a guy and I really saw the face of my mum at the window, but she had been fast asleep at the time. Did I imagine it all or was it my guardian angel? I don't know how else to explain his shock and surprise, which helped me escape.

There's no doubt in my mind that Sally experienced something supernatural that night and I emailed her back to say I believed her guardian angel had appeared to her in the guise of her mum. Remember, her mum was asleep at the time and when we sleep our spirits can soar.

The love of a parent also features in this next story from Helen.

Stunned

This happened eight years ago, at Christmas, and it still sends shivers down my spine when I think about it. It was a Saturday night and I was watching *Casualty* on TV as usual. For no reason at all I heard the voice of my dad telling me to get off my backside. He always used to yell at me like that when I still lived at home and was sitting watching TV. My dad's one of those very active people. He hates the telly. I can't say I watch that much, but after a busy day it's a real treat to sit down and relax. I'm getting sidetracked from my story now because what happened next will freak you out.

As I said, I was watching telly and I heard my dad yelling at me. Even though I'd left home years earlier my instinctive reaction was to do what my dad told me, so I got up. His voice felt so real, it was as if he was there in my house, but of course he wasn't. He was with my mum at their house five miles away, probably doing some DIY or something. It was very odd but as I stood there wondering what on earth was going on the mirror on my living-room wall suddenly fell down smashing into pieces on the sofa – the sofa where I had just been sitting.

I shudder to think what might have happened if I had been sitting there. I phoned my dad and told him about it and he couldn't believe it either, but all that I am telling you is true.

I have absolutely no doubt that Helen was telling me the truth and I have read or heard about many other stories relating similar last minute and totally unexplained warnings from the other side. Ten or so years ago when I first started researching and writing up stories for my angel books, one of the very first stories to come to my attention was this well-publicised one about a lady called Maria Tejada. Like Helen, Maria was relaxing at home when she was suddenly stunned to hear a familiar voice, warning her to get off her couch immediately.

Ghost of a chance

The voice of her dead dad prompted mother of six, Maria Tejada, to jump off her couch and as she did a speeding car smashed into her living room, crashing into the sofa where she had moments ago been sitting.

Maria believes that without her late father's warning she would not have stood a ghost of a chance. She described herself as the 'luckiest person in the world'.

After she heard her father's voice, Maria had run into her daughter's room. Seconds later a 1982 Chevy with two teens on their way to school crashed through the front door, ploughed into the couch and destroyed an interior wall. Everything in the living room and kitchen was smashed. Her house looked like a bomb had hit it, but Maria was just thankful to be alive and even more thankful that none of her children were at home. She was so relieved and believes that her father in spirit warned her and saved her life, just in the nick of time. She is quoted as saying: 'Dad loved me very much when he was still alive. I know that he must love me still because he saved me. He just didn't want me to die.' Mercifully, there were no deaths or injuries related to the crash and the driver of the car told police that his brakes had failed and the Chevy had simply spun out of control.

It's astonishing that Maria's departed father warned her in this way. Clearly it was not her time to die. And for the people in this next batch of stories it clearly wasn't their time to die either. I've grouped them together here because they all happened to drivers.

Let's begin with this intriguing story sent to me by Mark.

Never felt so frightened

Last winter I was driving on a frosty morning. I was going slowly and carefully around a bend but I still got into a skid. The car went this way and that, doing complete circles, and eventually came to a halt when it hit the kerb. When I looked up there was a line of traffic coming in the opposite direction that had completely stopped because they had obviously seen what was happening to me. I didn't have a scratch on me and my car wasn't damaged. I've never felt so frightened in all my life. How on earth did all those oncoming cars stop in time? I was brought up as a Roman Catholic but over the years I've been quite bad about attending mass regularly. However, one prayer I have never stopped saying several times a day is my guardian angel prayer. I really feel that my guardian angel looked after me that morning and I will be forever grateful.

And we'll follow on with this one sent to me by Charlene.

Don't move

Two years ago I was in my car driving to the supermarket to do some shopping when I came to a set of traffic lights at a major junction. There were roadworks taking place at the time. I was the first one at the lights and the light went green. I took my foot off the brake and was about to hit the accelerator when I heard a clear voice inside my head say, 'Don't move.' It was so distinct I thought someone was shouting to me from outside the car. I looked around me and checked my mirrors but there was no one there. By now there were cars hooting behind me so I knew these other drivers thought I ought to be moving, but just at that moment a lorry full of hot cement ran straight through the red light. It was astonishing. If I had not delayed for a few seconds I could well have been killed by the truck and if that had not killed me the hot cement might have. I believe it was my guardian angel or perhaps the guardian angel of the person in the car behind me, because if my car had missed the truck it would almost certainly have ploughed into the car behind me or the one behind that.

Ross had a similar experience.

Get over

I can't believe I am writing to you and if you had asked me six months ago about angels I would have laughed at the idea. I'm not religious, never have been, so you can imagine my surprise and shock when the voice of an angel saved my life, and more importantly the life of my precious children.

I was driving on the motorway. It was getting late and my four-year-old daughter and six-year-old son were both fast asleep in the back seat. I was driving along and I heard my daughter say, 'Get over, Daddy.' I looked at her in my rear-view mirror and she was still asleep, but for reasons I can't explain I decided to move over anyway. Within moments a car going in the opposite direction flashed past us at what must have been at least ninety miles an hour. If we had still been in that lane I believe we would all have died.

I've talked to friends and family about my experience and, like me, they all struggle to explain it but after reading your book it made perfect sense. My guardian angel used the voice of my little girl to get me to change lanes in the nick of time. He used her voice because she's a real daddy's girl, has me wrapped around her little finger and I'm accustomed to doing what she tells me. As I said, I didn't believe in miracles, but I think I do now.

I can relate to Ross's feelings of surprise and wonder because this is exactly how I felt when something comparable happened to me twelve years ago. At the time I was pregnant with my son. I was due to attend a radio interview and was driving towards a busy junction when I got stuck behind two slow-moving trucks. When I got to the junction both trucks indicated left, which frustrated me because that was the direction I needed to head in. I was just about to turn left behind them when I heard the voice of my departed mum speaking to me quite clearly. She told me to take the right-hand turn and, as was the case for Ross, for reasons I cannot explain I could not ignore the voice. I turned right, had to take a massive detour to get to the radio station and not surprisingly missed my interview. When I headed home that day I felt frustrated and angry to have missed such an opportunity to promote my writing, but later that evening when I turned on the news, feelings of anger melted into feelings of bewilderment and awe. I heard that there had been a terrible crash seconds after the two trucks had turned left at the junction. A stray dog had run into the road between the two trucks, causing the driver to slam on his brakes. There were three fatalities that day – the driver of the truck and the dog were unharmed but two passengers in the car behind and one in the car behind them had died on impact.

I believe that by telling me to take the right-hand turn, the voice of my mother in spirit saved my life that day. I had not expected to find proof of an afterlife but I had been given it all the same.

So far we've seen how the voice of an angel can intervene to prevent almost certain tragedy, but this next story sent in by Sheila takes things one stage further – or should I say higher?

Out of my hands

Every time I tell this story I get goose bumps. It was such a close call. I know when I tell it that I shouldn't really be alive to tell it at all. I was driving with my three friends; one was in the front seat and the other two were in the back. My friend in the front seat had her seatbelt on, as did I, but the two in the back had forgotten. We were all chatting and laughing when suddenly a car cut in front of us and the car we were in flipped over not once, but TWICE! Then it skidded across the road and into a tree. The front windows were broken and there was glass everywhere. When the car stopped I was in deep shock and so was my friend in the front seat beside me. I was certain that my friends in the back would be injured or dead – without seatbelts on there was no way they could have survived – but when I looked around they were absolutely fine. There was not a scratch on them. In fact, apart from a couple of bumps and bruises we were all absolutely fine.

My friends told me that they thought I had saved their lives with my brilliant driving skills while the car was flipping and skidding around. They said my calm control under pressure had saved the day. I hadn't freaked out and had taken charge of the situation. I told them this wasn't the case, but they wouldn't believe me and told me I was just being humble. I disagree. I mean, I'd be the first to take credit if it really had been me but hand on heart I am telling you that as soon as that car cut across mine, what happened next was out of my hands. Sure, my hands were on the wheel but I wasn't steering. Someone else was, someone else took over. I believe that someone was my guardian angel.

Sheila believes that her guardian angel took over on that day and I've heard this kind of thing said many times before, especially when it comes to automobile accidents. Let's follow on here with Radley's incredible experience.

Beat the light

Two years ago – but it seems like yesterday as I write this to you now – I was approaching a set of traffic lights. I saw that the signal was on amber and I figured if I sped up I could get through before it turned red, as I was running late for an appointment. I noticed that on the other side of the traffic lights there was a blue van waiting for its light to turn green.

At that moment I got the surprise of my life. I tried to put my foot down and go faster but the car would not respond. It felt as if invisible hands were stopping it from moving. Chills ran down my spine when I saw the blue van hurtle past me at speed. If I had done what I'd intended and tried to beat the light, it would have been a head-on collision. It's still a source of great amazement to me that an unknown force saved my life that day. It moves me deeply and feels like a miracle because two weeks later my girlfriend told me she was pregnant and I was about to become a dad for the first time. If I had died my son would never have known his father, and I'd never have known the miracle of becoming a father. To think I nearly lost it all because I was worried about being a few minutes late.

Again we hear phrases you may recognise from a few stories now – 'it still feels like it happened yesterday', 'reasons I cannot explain', 'an unknown force'. Virtually all the people who write in to me say that when angels dip into their lives, changing them or saving them, the event is remembered with vivid clarity. Even if the event happened many years ago, it stands out like a single bright star in a dark sky. It is impossible to forget because for reasons the people cannot explain events were taken out of their hands. For the person concerned the only explanation is that a higher power was involved. Shirley certainly feels this way:

Night shift

It was about ten o'clock in the evening and I was heading out for my night shift. I'm a nurse and I'd worked nights for the past three years so my body clock had really adjusted to being awake at night. I guess what I'm trying to say is I wasn't falling asleep or feeling sleepy at the wheel. As I approached the entrance to the hospital a car pulled out right in front of me. I reacted quickly and to avoid hitting it I was forced into another lane where a people carrier was heading straight towards me. It was impossible for three cars to be passing down this road side by side without an accident and I braced myself. I closed my eyes, let go of the steering wheel and prepared to die. But nothing happened.

A second or so later I opened my eyes and saw that I had passed between the two cars – one on my right and the other on my left. It was absolutely impossible. My car isn't huge, but it isn't that small either and the car that cut in front of me was fairly large, as was the people carrier. If you saw the road you would know that what happened was impossible. Even the most highly skilled driver would not have been able to do it. I looked in my rear-view mirror at the car driving behind me and then looked at the one driving ahead and they both flicked their lights to me, as if to say, 'How did we do that?' It was awesome but it was nothing to do with my driving and everything to do with my guardian angel. I know that an angel drove my car for me, saving not just my life, but the lives of the people in the other two cars. There is no other way I could have driven through those cars and I am eternally grateful as there's so much more living for me to do.

Jenny's story follows on here.

First past the post

I was on a steep hill heading towards a junction when my brakes failed. I panicked, as you might expect, as there was a lot of traffic on the road across the junction. There was no way I could stop my car in time and not crash into the vehicles on the other side. I was terrified and prayed, even though I'm not a religious person. I begged for a miracle. It wasn't just my own life I was scared of losing; I couldn't bear to be the reason for other people losing theirs.

I braced myself for the moment of impact but amazingly, astonishingly, as my mind blanked out with fear and terror my car made it through the heavy traffic on both sides, missed a lamp-post and a brick wall and eventually stopped in someone's front garden. They weren't best pleased, as I destroyed some treasured plants, but when you think of what might have happened and how incredible my escape was it puts it all in perspective. I don't know whether I blacked out or not, but whatever happened, it was a miracle. Someone drove my car that day like a Formula One driver and it wasn't me.

I'm placing Olivia's story here because it shows that angelic intervention might be more common than you'd think.

Just no way

This happened last winter, in January 2010, when we had that really cold spell. I shouldn't really have been out and about because there had been regular traffic warnings throughout the morning and I was only heading out to pick up some dry-cleaning, so it was hardly an essential journey. I was approaching a stop sign when I hit a patch of black ice. I didn't see it coming at all. I slammed my brakes on but they didn't seem to work. They were next to useless. The stop sign was there for a reason because if I didn't stop I would plunge into a busy road and be at the mercy of unsuspecting oncoming traffic.

I needed to turn right at the stop sign and I saw two cars on either side on the main road. They were both going to hit me and I was going to crash. With my brakes giving out on me, I could do nothing but brace myself for what lay ahead. An accident was unavoidable and it was anybody's guess if I would survive.

If I step back into that chilling moment I can remember feeling intensely alive. It was as if every cell in my body was vibrating and every nerve was throbbing. With my eyes shut I felt as if bolts of light were shooting through me. I thought I must be dead but when I opened my eyes I was very much alive. I was also sitting in a parked car; a car that was neatly parked a few inches behind the stop sign. It was impossible. My brakes had failed and I had let go of the wheel, but not only had my car stopped in time, it had stopped in exactly the right place.

I sat there for several minutes before another car came up behind me and started hooting loudly. The driver got out of the car and started swearing at me but I just smiled at him. I told him that I had just been staring death in the face and nothing he said could intimidate me. My out-of-this-world reaction clearly shook him up and he quietly got back into his car and drove around me to get out.

It was a good half an hour before I was able to move on. I talked to many other people trying to get past me and some clearly thought I was losing my mind, but a few others told me that it must have been an angel. I believe them. I wasn't imagining it. Eventually I called the AA and it turns out my brakes were busted – a cable had broken – and there is no way my car could have stopped like that without someone or something helping me out.

I've heard a number of stories now which describe the phenomenon of control over a potentially dangerous situation seemingly being taken out of a person's hands or, as Olivia described in her story above, unseen hands moving a person away from danger, or even steering the wheel or driving the car, as was the case in many of the other stories. Every time I read stories like that it reminds me of something I witnessed when I was a child. I first shared this story in one of my earlier books, *An Angel On My Shoulder*, and I'd like to revisit it with you now.

Follow that car

One day – I must have been about seven at the time – my mother picked me up from school and told me we were going to drive out of town to visit a dear friend of hers in hospital; her friend had suffered a stroke and, as I would discover later, had only days to live. We drove for about half an hour and then Mum must have missed a turning because it soon became clear we were heading in the wrong direction. Although I was young, I sensed how important it was for Mum that we got to see her friend that evening. It didn't help that it was midwinter and the weather was extremely bad with thick fog that refused to budge. The roads were fairly quiet but driving was still hazardous. Mum could barely see the markings on the road.

Suddenly the car's steering wheel jerked in Mum's hands and she lurched from the slow lane of the dual carriageway into the fast lane to overtake a car travelling ahead of us. As she overtook the car she came dangerously close to bumping into it and this uncharacteristically bad driving forced the car in the slow lane to swerve. Understandably infuriated, the driver hooted his or her horn several times and, obviously still angry, proceeded to overtake us via the slow lane before cutting in front of us in the fast lane.

Unaware of just how hazardous Mum's erratic driving had been I found it all wildly exciting. As we watched the car speed off and disappear in the fog ahead of us I asked Mum if she was going to play catch-up and 'follow that car'. She shook her head and told me she needed to stay in the fast lane, but this didn't mean she had to drive really, really fast.

By now we were approaching a roundabout and the fog was getting really thick. I looked out of the window and saw the hazy figures of two people frantically pushing a car from the slow lane to the side of the road. The stalled car was moving but as we drove past it was still blocking much of the slow lane. If we had stayed in the slow lane we would have almost certainly slammed into it because the fog was so heavy and the car being pushed out of the road had no lights on. My mum slowed to a crawl as we passed by with her emergency lights flashing to warn cars coming behind and we watched the car being pushed off the road, relieved that it was no longer a threat to oncoming traffic in the slow lane. We were just about to speed up again when there, shining in the head-lights, my mum noticed a nearly concealed sign pointing us in the right direction to the hospital.

Later my mum told me that her guardian angel drove her car that day and that it had not been her hands at the wheel. She said that very same angel made sure she found a sign to direct her to the hospital to see her friend one last time. She also told me that an angel saved not just our lives as we headed to the hospital but the lives of the people in the stalled car and the life of the driver with road rage. She explained that angels can manifest themselves in the most unusual and unexpected ways. If her guardian angel hadn't made her overtake the car ahead and make the driver angry, he or she would have stayed in the slow lane and crashed. I believed her and still believe her to this day.

So far voices and unseen hands have featured in our automobile stories, but this next story sent in by Aliesha offers even more than that.

Green light

I was driving home on 14 January 2004, and I remember putting my foot down because I wanted to make it through a green light before it changed. Then out of the blue a van appeared and hit the passenger side of my Mini. I recall the accident happening in slow motion. I didn't lose consciousness but I knew I was injured because I could feel blood trickling down my head. Then I felt the blood being wiped away by a lady with green hair – yes, green: make of that what you will. She was in the passenger side of my car. She told me not to panic and that an ambulance would arrive soon to take care of me. She was right because minutes later the police came, closely followed by paramedics. As soon as they arrived I turned away from the green-haired lady to talk to them and tell them I was OK, shaken but OK, and when I turned back the lady had gone.

Later, I told the police and the paramedics about the lady in the passenger seat but they told me it would have been impossible for anyone to get in or out, the passenger side of my car was so badly crushed. There was only one witness, the driver of the van, and he hadn't seen anyone either. My doctor told me I had probably been hallucinating with the shock but after reading some of the stories in your book I'm not so sure. I know in my heart what I saw and she was someone – something – wonderful. Could she have been my guardian angel?

Stephen also wrote to me to ask if he had met his guardian angel behind the wheel. Here's his story.

Running on empty

I was driving to a business meeting in a remote part of Scotland and got very lost. This was about thirty years ago in the days before satnav and before we all had mobile phones. It was getting dark and my visibility was poor because it was starting to snow. My car started to splutter and I realised that I would soon be out of petrol, completely in the middle of nowhere. Stupidly I'd forgotten to fill up in the morning. The roads were deserted and I started to panic, but then to my great relief I saw a car parked on the side of the road with its headlamps on.

I stopped alongside it and asked the man inside if he could help me. I explained my situation – I was lost and out of petrol – yet he asked me how much petrol I had left in my tank. I told him it was empty but he didn't seem to believe me because he got out of his car and peered inside mine to check. Then he told me my car had a good ten miles left in it and he was heading to a petrol station about six miles away. I could follow behind him. I told him I didn't think I could make it but he laughed and said I would be fine. Something about this guy made me trust him – I thought he must be a mechanic or something as he really seemed to know about cars – so I cranked up my engine again until it finally started. Then I followed him slowly for several miles.

It was starting to snow very heavily now. My petrol gauge was on empty and I kept expecting my car to grind to a halt but it kept staggering on. Eventually, we came to a steep hill. I got scared again because I knew the hill would eat up all my petrol and I didn't fancy skidding backwards when it finally ran out, but the guy flashed his lights ahead of me as if he sensed my nerves. Then he put his hand out of the window and waved his arm to encourage me to go forward.

Against my better judgement I started to head up the hill, following in his tyre tracks. It was terrifying but I managed reach the top and when I did I saw the welcoming lights of a petrol station about fifty feet away. I wanted to catch up with the guy to thank him for leading me to safety but as I reached the top of the hill the tyre tracks disappeared. They were not covered by fresh snow. They had just gone. I had only been a few feet behind him when he drove to the top of the hill but there were no tracks leading ahead or to the left or right. No tracks at all. He had just disappeared, along with his car.

I drove to the garage and filled my car with petrol. My thoughts were racing. When I got back inside my car I grabbed the handbook and read the section on the petrol gauge. It did not take me long to figure out that when the petrol gauge hit empty there was no way my car should have continued to run as long as it had done. I also tried to remember the guy and I realised that I could not recall anything about him – what he was wearing, his hair colour or even the sound of his voice. I couldn't remember what his car looked like either – everything about him and his car had just disappeared from my mind.

Even though it is decades later I still get a tingly feeling when I write down this story. I just cannot explain what happened to me. I'm not the kind of person to make things up – anyone who knows me can testify to that – and up until then I did not believe in angels. Obviously, I do now. How could I not?

Stephen's intriguing story is yet more powerful testimony that angels don't always conform to the traditional image of wings and halo. They can also manifest in the most ordinary of ways and it is only after the event that the person realises they may have encountered someone extraordinary.

Here's yet another breathtaking automobile story sent to me by Kirstie:

Angel wings

I was driving my car. It was dark and all of a sudden my headlights went out. I could hear a lot of noise and sparking from the engine. I knew it was a no stopping zone but my first instinct was to get out of the car as fast as I could. Then just as I was about to stop I knew it was all over because a large white bus hit my car. I closed my eyes and heard a swishing sound but when I opened them again and looked up I was fine. I could not believe it. For a moment I thought I was dead and I was simply watching the scene unfold. But I wasn't dead. The bus had pulled up alongside of my car and the driver was shouting at me. I think he too was shaken up by what had happened because he thought he had killed me. I couldn't say anything to him; I was just in shock.

The noise I heard had sounded like angel wings covering me as the bus ran into me. As long as I live I will never forget that night. I was pregnant at the time with my son and it terrifies me to think that I might not only have lost my life but lost him as well.

Kirstie is convinced an angel saved his life and who are we to argue otherwise? In much the same way, who are we to disagree with Natasha, whose story is below. Natasha's story differs from Kirstie's in that, although it involves cars, it did not take place behind a wheel but is similar in that Natasha also feels there is no other possible explanation for her miraculous escape.

The force was with me

I was walking to pick up my children from school. When I approached the main road I had to cross I looked both ways and saw that there was not a car in sight. I was about to step onto the road when I suddenly felt as though someone was behind me and pulling me backwards – with such force that I almost lost my footing. I was stunned when I looked around as there was no one there. I tried again to walk across the road but the force pulled me back again. It was as if someone had a hold of my arm and was pulling me backwards.

Just then I heard a loud screeching sound. I looked up and saw a young drunk driver driving at ridiculous speeds down the road. He was driving so fast and seemed to have come out of nowhere.

I realised that it was my guardian angels who were pulling me out of the road. If I had crossed the road at that point I would have been hit by the mad driver and almost certainly killed. I felt shaken up, and thanked my angels for their help and their warning.

My angels send me little signs like this all the time, trying to warn me or give me guidance or advice. If there are things that are extremely important for me to remember then sometimes they help me by making a flash of light by the calendar so I go and check it, or if I am feeling angry or upset then I hear comforting words being said to me or feel a warm feeling of calmness come over me.

I have had animals warn me of things and my angels also warn me or remind me about things through songs, people and things I see and feel.

Moving away from highways to beaches, Amber is also convinced angels are watching over her.

Angel in the sea

I was on holiday with a couple of friends in Barbados. A week had passed and we still had another week to go. It really was like paradise. I'd spend my days sinking in the dazzling white sand and gazing at the turquoise waves calling me in for a soothing swim. I didn't want this holiday to end.

One morning I napped a little too long in the sun and when I woke up I felt in urgent need of a cooldown. I woke up my mates and urged them to come into the sea with me but they were intent on topping up their tan. I laughed and ran into the waves. I settled into a steady backstroke for a few minutes but then, as I turned round to practise my front crawl, I felt a rush of cold water swirl around me. I'd been caught by a current and it was pulling me under. Struggling to keep my head above the water, I tried to shout and wave to my friends. To my horror they simply waved back; they thought I was larking about.

The current was too strong for me. My head went under again and again. I was being swept away to sea. My friends had finally realised what was happening and I glimpsed them running for help. But I knew I was beyond help. No one would be able to get to me in time. I sank under the water and images flashed through my mind. I was at school. I was opening Christmas presents. I was passing my driving test. I was in my job interview. I saw my parents. Even though I was under water I cried out that I wasn't ready to die. My life had barely begun.

I felt a strong arm grip my waist and pull me to the surface. I turned around and saw a middle-aged woman with silver hair supporting me. She told me to swim and out of nowhere I felt the strength returning to my legs. Slowly but surely I swam to shore. I could see my friends swimming towards me, shock etched onto their faces. They grabbed me and pulled me out of the sea. They were in shock because they thought that I had drowned. I turned around to thank my silver-haired saviour but she wasn't there. I asked my friends to tell me where she had gone; I was worried she might be in trouble. But the sea was still and empty. I asked them if they had seen her save my life but they shook their heads and told me they hadn't seen anyone.

As I sat on the sand shivering and chattering about a mysterious woman I'm sure my friends thought I was simply in a state of shock but I know different. I thought about the calm and strong woman who had saved me and a feeling of great peace, calm and strength bolted through me. I realised then that it hadn't been a human being who had saved me but an angel. It wasn't my time to die that day.

From that day on my life changed completely. When I came back I knew that my destiny was to help save the lives of others. I retrained as a paramedic. There are many lives, of course, that I can't save in my job, but for those that I do save and for those that I don't, I know that an angel is watching.

Amber thought her life was ending that day but now believes it was only beginning. She was drowning and her friends would not have been able to get to her in time to save her, but an angel was watching over her.

But why?

I'm pretty sure as you read stories such as Amber's that a part of you is still trying to reconcile why some people are given help, comfort or warning in times of danger by the angels and others are not. In short, why are some people saved and others not? I raised this burning issue earlier in the chapter but I'm fully aware that the response I initially gave – that our human minds simply cannot understand the divine plan – is one that you may be tired of hearing or perhaps not feel comforted or reassured by. If this is how you feel I'd like to take this opportunity to ask you if you are *really* sure you want an explanation. Do you really want to know why the innocent suffer? You may just find that it is infinitely preferable to keep asking the questions than to know the answers.

Of course, the fact that innocent people suffer without cause upsets you. I'd be shocked if it didn't, because anyone with a shred of sensitivity in their heart should be disturbed by the cruelty and unfairness in the world. Anyone who sees or reads or hears about injustice of any kind should find it hard to get their head and their heart around it. But let me ask you this: What if your guardian angel appeared to you right now and gave you all the answers? What if you had an explanation and knew why the innocent suffer?

In my humble opinion, knowing the answer would be an even greater tragedy than not knowing it because it would desensitise us to the suffering of others. And that would make the world a terrible and cold place to live in. Instead of wanting to help the innocent who suffer, we would watch their suffering without compassion or empathy or the desire to help or comfort them. You may not believe it, but that is what would happen if we knew why distressing things happened to good people. We would know why they were in distress and as a result we would not feel compassion for them. One example that immediately springs to mind is when a woman is giving birth and howling with pain when each contraction comes. Her loved ones and friends, however, aren't typically that concerned or troubled by her screams because they know it is perfectly normal. Quite the opposite, in fact − if it is a routine delivery and no complications have been detected they are excited and full of joy because she is about to have a baby.

In other words, when you understand the distress and pain of someone else, it is easier to deal with it. When we know why someone is suffering, we aren't so distressed by it. And by extension if you knew why innocent people have to suffer, if you could make sense of tragedy, injustice and cruelty, in time you would learn to deal with it. We would see news reports of starving people in developing countries and not be so moved by their suffering. We could bear the cry of a child in pain and not be inspired to comfort it. We could witness injustice and cruelty and not be horrified. We could accept pain and distress because we could understand why cruel things happen and explain them to ourselves. With the big 'why' questions answered, we could go about our daily routines totally unmoved.

However, as long as the suffering of others moves us we will remain distressed by its existence and inspired to ease or end it. Unable to rationalise their pain, we try to do all we can to ease it, and if that isn't possible we can open our hearts to them and pray for them to find comfort, strength and hope. So, perhaps the best thing is for us to keep on asking the 'why do good people have to suffer' question, but to stop wasting energy trying to find an answer. Instead, we should use our feelings of outrage and frustration and transform them into positive action by helping those who suffer and fighting unfairness and injustice whenever and however we can. In short, we can prove with our hearts and our actions that the forces of love and goodness are indeed more powerful than the forces of evil and darkness.

We shouldn't sit back and expect our guardian angel to do all the work for us. Sure, on rare occasions they may – again for reasons we cannot understand – choose to intervene. But, as I always stress, this is very rare. More often than not they will not interfere with our choices and decisions, even if these choices and decisions lead us onto the wrong path. This is because we have been given the sacred gift of free will, the blessing of choice, and heaven is waiting for us to choose light instead of darkness, to trust in eternal life even when everything seems dark and hopeless. The angels are waiting for us to make this positive choice not just once in our lives, but every day, every moment, because that is our purpose in life. The only way for us to grow spiritually is to combat injustice, pain and cruelty with love and goodness.

We don't need answers, we don't want the mystery to be solved, what we really want and need is more compassion, kindness and love to put an end to our suffering. That is the reason for our existence. It is why we are born and why we live.

CHAPTER THREE

Miraculous Escapes

They will lift you in their hands so that you shall not strike a foot against a stone.

Psalm 91: 12

When it is dark enough you can see the stars.

Ralph Waldo Emerson

When this book is published the year 2012 will be just around the corner (or if you are reading this later, it will be already upon us or behind us) and if you believe what some people say, every last one of us will be in need of some kind of miraculous escape, because the world is going to end!

Are you scared?

Don't feel like you are all alone if you feel a little apprehensive. Even those who dismiss the 2012 predictions as scaremongering with no basis in fact may, at times, even if they never admit it, feel a little apprehensive and uncertain. They may well have good reason.

About twelve years ago I first stumbled upon the 2012 doomsday theories. At first, like many others, I dismissed the predictions as silly nonsense, but the rumours persisted. Eventually, my curiosity as a paranormal writer and researcher got the better of me and I began to dig a lot deeper. The first thing I noticed was that finding reliable information about 2012 can be difficult. There are so many sources claiming different things, and the media can't always be trusted either. You probably know some of these, if not all, but let me give you an overview of the most popular 2012 theories:

- The Mayan calendar is an ancient calendar which ends on 21 December 2012. The Mayans have accurately predicted many events, and so people are worried about what this means.
- The Chinese I-Ching prophecies also predict the end of the world on this exact date, which is interesting considering there is no way people living in those ancient times on opposite sides of the Earth would have been able to communicate.
- Prophecies made by Nostradamus among others also predict great disasters in the year 2012.
- The Bible Code, which is a method for discovering hidden messages in the Bible, has predicted events with great accuracy. The Bible Code also predicts major catastrophes in the year 2012.
- The planet Nibiru or Planet X is predicted to arrive in 2012. On this planet there are living beings called the

Anunnaki, and what they are planning to do nobody knows. What we do know, however, is that if planet Nibiru is real and if it enters our solar system, then there may be great climatic catastrophes on Earth.

These were just some of the predictions for this year and they all sound pretty frightening. I'd only researched the 2012 phenomenon for a week when I started to get apprehensive. Indeed, feeling scared began to feel natural considering all the frightening doomsday predictions I was reading about. Few other dates in history have had this kind of doomsday speculation attached to them.

Over the years I've been asked many times how I interpret predictions that the world, as we know it, will end on 21 December 2012. And now with 2012 so close – or if you buy this book later than publication, already upon or behind us – I've noticed a huge increase in the number of questions coming in. Here's a snapshot of some of them:

Will there be global war — possibly triggering a nuclear holocaust?

Will the planet's life forms finally succumb to the ecological quagmire that's been building in our soils, oceans and atmosphere?

Will the current steady increase of previously unknown diseases overcome our ability to defend against them?

Should I be preparing myself for the end?

What should I tell my children?

Do you think this is all scaremongering nonsense?

Are you scared?

I wrote back to everyone who contacted me to say that although I was scared at first I'm not scared any more. Quite the opposite, in fact − I'm excited because it is my personal conviction that 2012 isn't about the world ending, but about a crucial turning point in humankind's spiritual development.

I truly believe that the year 2012 is a central point in the evolution of our spiritual perception. I dismiss all those theories that suggest 2012 is the end of the world as, in my opinion, none have real evidence. However, my conviction that human awareness is altering does have solid evidence and that evidence is the growing number of spiritual experiences and insights of ordinary people, like you and me, from all religions, cultures and walks of life. Some of these people, like Sally whose story is below, admitted that they were perhaps the last people you would expect to claim such things.

Helping hand

I wasn't exactly what you might call a spiritual person. Even when my husband, Luke, died from the devastating effects of prostate cancer I didn't draw any comfort from well-meaning souls who told me he was at peace now in the afterlife. I didn't believe in the afterlife. I thought when we died that was it.

Miraculous Escapes

At Luke's funeral I felt tired and empty more than anything else. I missed him terribly and now I would have to face the future without him. It wasn't fair, but then I have always known and accepted that life isn't fair. The funeral was bad enough but the deafening silence after all the well-wishers had gone proved to be far worse. I can recall exactly the moment I became an alcoholic and that was the night of his funeral.

Alcohol filled the empty place in my life that Luke had once filled. Prior to his illness we had been inseparable. We had spent our time working and living together and when we weren't working we went biking in the woods, singing in the choir or walking hand in hand. We loved spending all our time together. Just before he was diagnosed with cancer we had been talking about children but after five long years of his suffering I went into early menopause. I was widowed at forty-four but I felt like eighty-four.

I became very good at hiding my drinking. I don't think anybody ever knew but I'm sure they had their suspicions when I started to turn up late and dishevelled at work. One night about five months after Luke died I was driving home from work. My head was sore, my eyes were heavy and all I could think about was having a drink. I turned the radio on and turned it up loud to keep myself awake. I was surprised that the song playing was Abba's 'I Have a Dream' – they were singing the line, 'I believe in angels, something good in everything I see.' I'd not heard it played on the radio before and it was the song Luke and I had both sung together when we first met.

Missing Luke, I wiped a tear from my face and could not believe what I smelled on my hands. I smelled Luke. It wasn't his aftershave or his medication. It was his distinctive smell – the smell I had adored before his illness. The smell I loved whenever I snuggled onto his chest. To my surprise my sadness was replaced by a feeling of joy. I knew then that Luke was with me, holding my hand every step of the way. How else could I smell him on my hands in my car? The song we had both sung when we first met was playing on the radio and Luke's scent was on my hands – the hands he used to hold.

My experience that night changed my life for ever – not only did I stop drinking but it was a launch pad to my belief in a world that goes on after we die. Although I know that Luke can never hold my hand physically, the touch of his hands and his scent will linger with me for ever. I know he is still with me. He never left.

Stories like these, which I receive in ever-increasing numbers every day, along with my own research and experience and the huge increase in interest in books, documentaries, TV shows and magazines about angels and the paranormal, make it clear to me that the barrier separating our physical world from the non-physical dimensions is weakening every day now. That barrier is largely created by our minds and the way in which we use our thoughts to form our perceptions of the world we live in.

I know this because before I opened my eyes to the world of spirit in my late thirties, I did not believe I would ever be able to see, hear, or feel my angels. Even though I now understand that my angels were all around me all along, my awareness blocked them out. I longed to be able to 'see' things but I never did. It wasn't until I understood that my preconceptions about what was and was not possible (along with a heavy dose of fear) were blocking them out that the veil between this world and the next began to lift. The human mind finds it impossible to deal with things that it believes to be impossible. Thankfully, we all have a tiny opening in this self-created barrier that prevents us from experiencing miracles. For me that opening was my vivid dreams and my empathy, a gift for relating to the feelings of others that every human being has and which is the first step towards psychic awareness. Fortunately, this gift opened other psychic doors for me and eventually brought me to the point I am at today, where my self-created shield against the invisible world has been shattered and my life has changed forever as a result.

The incredible numbers of people who are seeing angels has led me to believe that these people provide all the evidence we need for the dawning of a new era where the world of spirit is no longer laughed at or dismissed, but where it becomes something impossible to deny because it is a part of our everyday reality. Doomsday theorists may talk about natural disasters, melting icecaps and violence between nations, but none of these suggests to me that the world is at a crucial turning point as much as the stories people are sending me every day about their experiences with angels. If you look back at our history you will find it littered with natural disasters, ice ages and violence between cultures but you won't find people all over the world uniting in their belief in angels in the way they are today. The decline of religion and growth of the internet are certainly contributory factors here, along with the deep-seated spiritual longing that exists deep within each human being, but I also believe that the angels have chosen this moment in time to make themselves known as never before. I believe there is evidence that our perception of time is altering: a sort of karmic compression is occurring that speeds up the rate at which the consequences (good or bad) of our actions manifest in our lives – as witnessed by the huge popularity of recent books such as *The Secret*.

Whether the story is one of angels, ghosts, miracle healing, coincidences or any one of a myriad possible scenarios, all come from an increasing dynasty of people I call 'angel talkers.' The stories these people send in to me every day are real events. The sceptics can say what they will – but there is abundant information to prove that psychic powers are real and that miraculous events are happening to people every day; ordinary people all over the world are being saved by their angels.

Most of the stories you've read so far were sent to me by people living in the UK, but that is simply because I'm UK-based and so is my publisher and many of my books reach British readers first. However, I want to stress that I've gathered stories from all over the world proving that there is without doubt a universal belief in the idea of celestial beings watching over us. All these stories show that growing numbers of people from diverse cultural and religious backgrounds are attracted to the idea of angels saving us from danger and from ourselves. And the more people who believe in miracles, the more likely it is for them to occur in our everyday lives.

Whatever you think about 2012, there is no doubt that the number of people worldwide who are becoming more spiritually aware is steadily increasing. I'm not talking about religion here. I'm talking about spirituality, and there is a difference. Spiritually-minded people may or may not commit themselves to a certain religion, but what sets them apart is their ability to transcend religious, cultural and ethnic differences to see the oneness of all humankind and in this way they can bring love, goodness and, most important of all, heart and hope into the world. I truly think that belief in angels is uniting people all over the world and saving the world in the process. And perhaps this is the real secret of 2012? It won't be the end of the world but the dawning of a new age when angels transcend cultural, ethnic and religious differences and become a true uniting force. The dawning at long last of a new and magical age when the invisible world makes itself known to us through the voices of ordinary people with simple but extraordinary stories to tell.

And never before have we more badly needed to hear these voices. In a world still torn apart by injustice, poverty and cruelty, each angel story is a message of healing and hope that can rescue us from our past and guide us into the future: not the end of the world but a new dawn. Indeed every angel story is a miraculous escape and a new beginning in itself, because the more we focus on what is uplifting and inspirational, the closer the angels fly beside us.

I've certainly had a few miraculous encounters of my own, but even today this doesn't stop me wondering if the angel stories sent to me are real, a coincidence or only real to the people who sent them in. This wondering never bothers me, though, because in every case I come to the same conclusion – if an experience feels real to a person, so real that it saves lives or changes them for the better, it will cause even those with the most sceptical of minds to pause for a moment and wonder if angels exist. And every time someone pauses − even for the briefest of moments − to wonder if a higher power is guiding us in this way, it is a miraculous escape or, as I like to call it, a miracle.

And now that we have returned to the subject of miracles, I think you are going to be fascinated by this next group of astonishing stories. If you thought what you read previously was astonishing, brace yourself, because the ones that follow are truly out of this world. I'll plunge in right now with this one sent to me by Raj.

Blown away

Seven months ago I was involved in a car crash that completely destroyed my car and almost claimed my life. It was totally my fault as I fell asleep at the wheel, only to be jolted awake as my car spun around and jammed into a tree. Mercifully, there were no other vehicles involved. I remember not being able to see anything because there was so much smoke. I also remember not being able to breathe. I could hear a lot of bangs and mini explosions, though.

When the car finally stopped I was suspended upside down. I knew I had to turn the ignition off because the car was in danger of exploding with me trapped in it, but I didn't have the strength to move my hands. I was so weak with the lack of air. I tried to turn the key but I couldn't. I tried to open my door but again I was too weak. I could feel the life draining out of me and my eyes were burning. I really thought this was it. Either I would die from suffocation or the car

66

blowing up would kill me. Curiously, I don't remember feeling panic, just a kind of calm acceptance.

And then something incredible happened. I still can't believe it myself but I swear to you it is true. All of a sudden the key in the ignition turned off and the car door flew open, along with my seatbelt. Then I felt a pair of arms reach around me, lift me up and carry me through the air. I had this sensation of flying and the next thing I remember is lying well clear of the car as it blew up.

When the paramedics arrived I told them what had happened. I don't think they believed me, as there were no footprints at the scene and in any case it would have been physically impossible for a human to climb up and open the car door. When I told them I didn't think it was a human that saved me, they listened patiently but probably thought I was delirious from the gases and the shock of the explosion. I wasn't delirious, though, Theresa. I was weak and faint and there is no way I had the strength to get out of the car by myself. And even if I did somehow manage to get out, I had this sensation of flying to safety. It was incredible, like I was being rocked in a giant pair of arms.

The only explanation that makes sense to me is that an angel helped me escape and an angel carried me to safety.

Did an angel help Raj escape almost certain death or, as the paramedics on the scene that day clearly thought, did he somehow find the miraculous strength within himself to survive his ordeal? It's often hard to tell the difference because, in my humble opinion, both are miracles, but Raj lived through the experience and knows what he believes. Twice in his story he mentions this sensation of flying or being carried. It sounds incredible, but from my research I know that it is not as unusual an occurrence as you might think. I've gathered many stories from people who also report this sensation of being carried to safety by something or someone invisible. Elizabeth's story is another stunning example.

Uplifted

I was about thirteen years old at the time – I'm forty-seven now – but I can remember the experience as clear as day, and it has never faded. When it happened I was carrying a book in my hands and glancing at the pages while trying to walk down a long and steep staircase, so really it was an accident waiting to happen. I missed my footing, the book flew out of my hands and I knew for sure in that moment I was heading for a big and dangerous fall. I braced myself for pain but felt nothing. Instead of falling I found myself floating down the stairs, a few inches above them. I also heard music playing. I still to this day can't identify the instrument. It was a beautiful sound I have not heard before or since. I thought I must be dying. So this was what it felt like!

But no, I wasn't dying – instead I found myself sitting at the bottom of the stairs with my book still in my hand, the book that had flown out of my hands when I tripped. How did that happen?

At the time I do remember getting this tingly feeling all over, but I was young and more accepting of the unusual. I didn't really think about it too much. However, the older I have become the more I find myself returning in my mind to that moment. And the more I think about it the more I am convinced that my guardian angel caught me and carried me to safety.

This sensation of floating or flying that Elizabeth shares so eloquently here is something I have never experienced when I'm awake. However, when I fall asleep it's a different matter altogether. In my dreams I often find myself flying and it feels perfectly natural and the experience is very liberating. If you have ever flown in your dreams – and many people do – you'll know how empowering and uplifting it can feel. You feel on top of the world and are soaring to great heights. There's more about dreaming in chapter five, but if you are a high-flier in your dreams, just imagine how incredible the sensation must be if it happens when you have your eyes wide open!

Joy sent me this account. In it she describes how an angel literally picked her up.

Flying backwards

I was out shopping with my two friends and we were walking up to a big crossroads. The lights were green but before those lights there was a smaller crossing without any lights. I'm usually really observant but I was pretty tired and I think all I saw was the green lights ahead. I didn't pay attention to any traffic that might be coming across the smaller crossing.

I was just about to cross over when a Mini came around the corner driving way too fast. I'm going to describe what happened next in as much detail as I can, because even I can't make sense of it and sometimes I don't believe it, but it did happen. It did happen. I put my right foot forward to step into the road and in a split second I heard the screech of tyres and a loud horn. I also felt myself being lifted above the ground. I hovered for a brief moment and then found myself placed back on the pavement just as the Mini swished past my face. My friends were behind me but they had not seen what happened because they had stopped a few moments before to check their mobiles. They only saw me thrown back onto the pavement. Only I know I wasn't thrown, I was lifted up into the air and placed on the pavement.

Like Joy, Connor also believes he was lifted up by an angel. Here's what happened to him.

Losing control

I was riding my bike to work. I've done that for the past eleven years and I pride myself on being a safe and careful cyclist. I also pride myself on the speed I can bike, so I'll be honest and tell you that I was going pretty fast. I was going down a fairly steep hill when I felt my back tyre run over a stone or something and I lost control. I knew that the bike was going to topple over and I was going down.

Now, I've had a few falls in my time and they've been OK because I always wear a helmet but today was the one day that I completely forgot to bring it with me. You see, I had an important presentation that morning and my thoughts had been preoccupied with what I needed to remember to say. I left the house reciting my key points in my mind and made the stupid mistake of forgetting my helmet. It was only after I had been cycling for ten or so minutes that I remembered, and by then it was too late to go back. I didn't panic because I thought I knew the route well and there weren't any pitfalls ahead. How wrong I was!

Back to my fall: I could feel myself going down and then I felt a pair of hands – very soft hands – pick me up under my armpits. I felt the air race past me and it felt as if I was being lifted very high because I didn't feel any part of me touch the ground and the next thing I knew was that I was standing about a foot from my bike, which was lying on the ground.

Looking back, if I had fallen naturally my head would most definitely have hit the concrete very hard. I didn't have my helmet so I would have been seriously injured or even killed. I was shaken by the whole experience but then I read one of your books and I knew I had to tell you about it. Do you think it was my guardian angel?

I think you know what my answer to this question was. Of course, I believe it was the work of Connor's guardian angel. I also believe that something supernatural occurred in this next story sent to me by Sara.

Elevated

My husband is a keen fisherman. I hate fishing myself, but it was our twentieth wedding anniversary and I wanted to do something special for him so I booked us both on a day-long fishing trip at the lakes. It was a beautiful day and we'd been out in the hire boat for a few hours when we decided to dock and have a picnic lunch.

We were close to the dock when the boat suddenly nose-dived and water gushed in. This freaked us both out, especially my husband as he can't swim. Stupidly, we hadn't put our life jackets on because it was such a warm day and we felt perfectly safe. There seemed to be no one around so we were in serious trouble. Then the worst happened and the boat flipped over, tossing us overboard. I was OK within moments because I could swim but my husband was not; he was drowning. I swam over to him as fast as I could – which wasn't very fast as I was still wearing clothes and shoes and this weighed me down – but I did get to him. He clung to me and I tried to keep his head above water but he was panicking and started to pull me down too. I knew I wasn't strong enough to save us both and I felt myself getting weaker and weaker. I was just about out of energy when I felt my feet touch something sturdy and flat in the water below. It gave me stability and a chance to catch my breath and, most important of all, it helped me keep my husband afloat and both of our heads above water. I stood on this platform for a few minutes and screamed for help. After about three or four minutes a couple of men appeared and came to our aid, pulling us both to safety.

I was so lucky to have found that platform to rest my feet on because when I stood on it my head and most of my shoulders were raised out of the water. It wasn't big enough for my husband to stand on but it gave me a platform to hold him from. When I told the guys about the platform I had been standing on they told me there couldn't have been anything there because the water was a good fifty feet deep. One of them was so curious he even jumped back into the water to investigate. I directed him to the spot where I thought it was but he couldn't find it. It wasn't there. I think my guardian angel placed it there. I can't think of any other explanation.

This next story – which was widely reported in the media in January 2009 – doesn't feature elevation or 'being lifted', but it does have certain similarities because it features the sensation of being dragged, again by invisible hands – or should I say wings? If you didn't read about it at the time, here's a brief recap.

The hand of an angel

A British survivor of the fire horror in a Bangkok club that left sixty people dead has told how he was saved from death by the hand of an angel.

Twenty-nine-year-old Londoner Alex Wargacki collapsed and fell unconscious as fire raged through the Santika club in Bangkok, Thailand. The fire went on to kill sixty people and Alex believes that he could well have been one of them if it had not been for the hand of an angel.

Speaking from Bangkok's private Samitivej Hospital, Mr Wargacki told reporters: 'I felt myself going unconscious. I knew something was happening to my lungs. I could not breathe. I blacked out and fell to the floor.

'I woke up and heard this voice saying, "Come on. Come on this way." Then I felt myself being dragged towards an exit.

'Had it not been for this voice with the hand of an angel I would not be alive today.'

The Foreign Exchange trader, who lived in Bangkok for four years, suffered burns and smoke inhalation and was put on a respirator to help him breathe, but went on to make a full recovery.

At the time the story was circulated Alex's miracle escape prompted a lot of speculation. Did an angel save him or was it a fireman or another party-goer, guided by the angel within them? Once again it is very hard to tell the difference and especially in this case as, to date, I don't think anyone has come forward to identify themselves as Alex's rescuer.

Uncertainty about the identity of the saviour in this next story – again widely reported in the media, but this time in August 2010 – doesn't figure here.

Hugged to life

After a three-hour labour in a Sydney hospital grieving mother Kate Ogg was told by doctors that all hope was gone for her newborn son. The little boy was born prematurely at twenty-seven weeks and weighing just 2lbs, and doctors spent twenty minutes battling to get the tiny baby to breathe, but their efforts were futile.

'The doctor asked me if we had we chosen a name for our son,' said Mrs Ogg. 'I said, "Jamie," and he turned around with my son already wrapped up and said, "We've lost Jamie, he didn't make it, sorry."'

The baby was declared dead and the distressed mother was urged to say her final goodbyes, but Kate couldn't bring herself to let her tiny son go, not just yet.

'It was the worst feeling I've ever felt. I unwrapped Jamie from his blanket. He was very limp. I took my gown off and arranged him on my chest with his head over my arm and just held him. He wasn't moving at all and we just started talking to him. We told him what his name was and that he had a sister. We told him the things we wanted to do with him throughout his life.'

For the next two hours Mrs Ogg hugged, touched and spoke to her son. And then an extraordinary thing happened: the little boy began to show signs of life. It was just a gasp of air at first that was dismissed by doctors as a reflex action, but then the startled mother fed him a little breast milk on her finger and he started breathing normally. Five months later, with her son in perfect health, Mrs Ogg describes how she felt at the time.

'He started gasping more and more regularly. I thought, "Oh my God, what's going on?" A short time later he opened his eyes. It was a miracle. Then he held out his hand and grabbed my finger. He opened his eyes and moved his head from side to side. The doctor kept shaking his head saying, "I don't believe it, I don't believe it."'

You might be thinking that this isn't strictly speaking an angel story, but a heart-warming story of the love a mother has for her child and the life-enhancing power of touch. And you'd be right. On one level it is a beautiful tale of maternal love, but on another level it is so much more than that, because it shows how in certain circumstances, love – and remember love is where angels can be found – can work miracles. It also shows that although humans are not angels – because angels are pure spiritual beings who have never lived on earth – they can sometimes be guided by a higher power to save or transform the lives of others. In much the same way, loved ones who have passed away are not angels as such, but they can be guided by our angels to give us comfort and support and, in some cases, life-saving miracles when we need them the most.

And sometimes it's not distressing circumstances or dangerous situations that we most need saving from, but ourselves, as
this next story, sent to me by David, illustrates so well.

From the brink

Those who suffer from depression will know that it is an ugly, dark
place to be. Looking back, it feels like I was born depressed. I can't
remember a time when I felt good about myself. It might have had
something to do with the fact that I was brought up in a care home,
or the fact that I've always been hugely overweight and hated the
way I looked. I don't know why I inherited the curse of depression,
but I did. Things reached crisis point when I was in my early thirties,
living alone in a bedsit and working in an office job I loathed. Around
this time I went from moderate to serious depression. I began experiencing panic attacks and other symptoms, like insomnia, paranoia
and constant bouts of illness. I need to tell you that it wasn't just
sadness that I experienced; it was a real, dark, empty existence.
Some days I would phone in sick at work and stay in bed all day. I
didn't feel anything but tiredness and heavy sadness.

One day after another endless, sleepless night I made the decision
to end it all. With a purpose I had not had before and an energy in
my step I was equally unfamiliar with, I went from chemist to chemist to buy an assortment of sleeping pills. Then I stopped at the
off-licence to stock up on alcohol. I didn't want to botch this up. I
wanted to do it properly.

So there I was, armed with pills and drink and ready to leave life
behind. It was a bitterly cold day, dark and dreary with the prospect

of heavy snow, and the harshness of the weather seemed to mirror the cold and stinging feeling in my heart. I was at an all-time low and I remember thinking that if ever there was a time for an angel to appear, now would be really good. I'd never been religious in any way so it surprised me that I would even think this, but I did think it all the same and the moment – the very moment – that the word angel crossed my mind, the sun broke through the clouds, warming my cold face. The heat was so strong that I stopped dead in my tracks. As the sunlight showered over me I felt myself getting warm from the inside. It was an incredible, unforgettable feeling. I was quite literally aglow.

While I was standing there a man stopped and asked me if I was OK. It was probably the first time somebody had asked me that in years. I looked at him and said I was just enjoying the sunlight. The man looked at me and said, 'What sunlight, mate? It looks pretty dark and dank to me. Are you sure you are OK?' I nodded and as I did I looked around and noticed that it was indeed dark and dreary again. The sunlight had gone. I asked the man if he had seen it and again he told me that he hadn't. Then he laughed and told me he envied me because I was obviously one of those glass-half-full kinds of people who try to make the best of everything – even hellish weather on a day like this. Then he went on his way.

For the next few minutes I stayed rooted to the spot, aware that something extraordinary was happening inside me. From that moment on I can honestly say that I have never felt so empty again. I started to change. Something in my spirit had been fed by that shaft of sunlight. I had discovered a joy inside me that was being reawakened. This isn't to say I have never had my off days, of course

I have, but I can cope with them now because I feel happy on the inside. I have discovered a comfort and a peace I didn't know I had.

All this happened over twenty years ago. I'm in my fifties now and I'm happily married with six children. I also went back to college and work as a counsellor. I want to give hope to people like me who struggle with depression. We have a wonderful healthcare system that can help with medication and counselling but I also understand and know from first-hand experience that healing comes from the angels within and around us.

Yes, depression is an ugly, empty and dark place to be, but even the most desperate and lonely of situations can be filled with feelings of love and hope.

Becky's story also shows how sometimes we just need rescuing from ourselves.

Pushed aside

This is the first time I have shared this story with anyone. For years I have buried it deep inside me. In many ways it has shaped and defined me. I'll begin at the beginning. I was twenty-one and grieving the death of my mother. I had been out with my boyfriend and had had quite a few drinks. I ended up fighting with him and he dumped me. He said he never wanted to see me again. I was very disorientated and distressed. I should have got a cab home because it was starting to rain and it was getting dark and cold but I didn't care. I just started walking and walking. At one point I remember crossing a fairly busy road. I stopped in the middle of it and felt all the pain in my heart. I'd lost my mum and now my boyfriend. It had always been just me and Mum and my boyfriend and now it was just me. I couldn't see much point in existing any more, so I just stood there and, like a rabbit caught in the headlights, waited for a car to hit me, take all the pain away. My legs couldn't move and I closed my eyes, but at that very instant I felt myself being shoved and pushed across the road so hard that I fell onto the pavement.

I looked up and saw this woman. She had brown hair and clear blue eyes. She didn't say a word but there was such a look of concern and love on her face that I knew I could trust her. She held out her hand and helped me stand. I started crying and before I knew it I was telling her all about my worries. As I talked she held my hand and gently rubbed my shoulder in exactly the same way Mum used to do when she was alive. It was the most comforting sensation. It gave me such strength. We started to walk home and I didn't stop talking and talking. The woman still didn't say a word, but it was like she didn't need to because I could feel her love and concern.

Eventually we got to my front door and I fumbled inside my handbag for my keys. When I looked up the lovely, kind lady had gone. I ran about a bit, calling for her, but she had quite literally vanished. I felt a bit shaken at first but then I thought about her clear, blue eyes and I felt calm again.

It's been four years since that night and every time I think about it I still get this wonderful feeling of comfort. The feeling is as strong as it was on the night. It never seems to fade from my heart. It is locked deep inside there and it never fails to guide and inspire me. Whether she was human or divine, an angel saved me that night and continues to save me to this day.

Becky isn't sure that it was an angel who saved her life, but what she does know is that whenever she remembers the compassionate soul who stepped forward with grace and courage that night, she discovers something miraculous and magnificent within herself. Just like Becky, I can't say for certain that unexplained, supernatural powers were involved in all the stories in this book, but what I can say for sure is that sometimes life-saving or life-changing miracles happen to ordinary people when they least expect them. And sometimes angels – either in their spiritual form or in the form of other people – can lift us up and carry us a while when the going feels just too hard for us to cope with alone. In the process they leave not just the person involved, but all who read or hear about their story, in a state of questioning wonder that can transform their lives for ever. This is exactly what happened to Evelyn.

Somewhere in time

In winter 2007 the love of my life – my husband of thirty-two years – died. Everything about my life changed in a way I hated. I didn't know who I was any more. We had always been like two halves of a whole – with my husband being the better half. I just didn't work without him. For weeks and months afterwards I didn't go out of the house; I couldn't face the world without him by my side. I needed to be surrounded by things that still smelled of him. I barely ate and if I needed anything I ordered it online and had it delivered to my door.

One night I thought I was going to die too. I went to bed with a horrible headache. It felt like my head was going to burst open. I thought that it was my time and in some respects I felt quite relieved and happy because perhaps I would be with my husband again.

I remember closing my eyes and thinking deeply about my husband. I begged him to come and get me; take me away with him to a better place, just as he had done when we first met. Suddenly, it felt as if he was sitting on the bed beside me. I didn't see him but I felt him put an arm around my shoulder and gently rock me. I felt blissfully, insanely happy. My time had come and I was going away at last with my husband.

The next thing I knew I was wide awake. My head didn't hurt any more and it was daylight outside. I looked at the clock beside my bed and it was ten o'clock in the morning. I had not slept in that long for over a decade. I was in for an even greater surprise when I turned on the television and noticed that I had skipped a day. I had gone to bed on a Sunday night and it was now Tuesday. I had slept for nearly forty hours. I knew then that I wasn't meant to die and be with my husband – not just yet. I had just needed a really good rest, a time-out. There were things I still needed to do.

And one of those things was to be there for my daughter and my son. I had been so wrapped up in my grief I hadn't realised how much they were hurting too. They had tried to contact me when I was in my self-imposed prison but I'd refused to let them in. I also got a part-time job working at my local library. I've always been a book lover and it's the perfect job for me. One of the things I enjoy most is taking the mobile library to visit people who for health reasons can't get out of their houses much. Although I wasn't physically ill when my husband died, I was emotionally ill, so I know how it feels when you can't get outside. Your world starts to shrink. It's very rewarding to see the eyes of the people I visit light up when I call round with my recommended reads for the month. They love telling me what they thought of a particular book or a reading choice I made for them. That's why I love books, you see: if you can't get out into the world, they can bring the world to you.

Evelyn never found out from her doctor what happened to her that night and why she slept for such an unusually long time, but she believes that long sleep saved her life. I like to think she met her husband in her dreams. Of course, you could explain it all away from a medical perspective but that doesn't in my opinion in any way lessen the value of this miracle.

The following story, filtered to the media in September 2010, could also be explained from a medical perspective, but in much the same way I don't think this takes a thing away from the wonder of it all. What do you think?

Back from the dead

Gore Otteson was submerged underwater for twenty-five minutes. Family members and doctors desperately tried to resuscitate him, but when his heart had stopped beating for over an hour, his family was told that he only had a one per cent chance of survival. But Gore did survive thanks to a fantastic medical team and, as his parents believe, a lot of prayer and someone watching over him.

Gore had been at the family's holiday home in the Rocky Mountains when disaster struck. His mother, Amy, was getting her two older children out of the bath before dinner. Her husband,

Dave, had returned to work in Denver that day but she had stayed in the cabin. While Amy was busy with the other children, Gore slipped out of the back door. When she realised he was missing, his mother began calling him and soon other family members who were staying in nearby cabins were searching for him too. After an agonising twenty minutes Gore was spotted trapped under a log in the fast-flowing irrigation ditch several hundred feet away from the cabin. Gore's grandfather immediately began CPR and continued until the paramedics arrived.

Gore was airlifted to Denver hospital where his heart was eventually restarted. Miraculously, Gore did not suffer any brain damage. His mother believes God heard her prayers and everyone involved described Gore's dramatic recovery as a 'miracle'.

Once again we hear the word 'miracle'. Yes, it is probably true that Gore would not have survived without a medical team working around the clock to revive him, and the prompt CPR given on the scene by his grandfather, but this remarkable story still has all the elements of a miracle, and Gore's mother is convinced that there is truly someone watching over her son.

Trisha's story didn't hit the newspapers in the same way, but I'm following with it here because it also involves a miraculous escape from drowning. Unlike Gore, who will probably never remember what happened to him as he was too young at the time, Trisha can recall every detail as if it had happened yesterday. What she shares with us now makes fascinating reading.

Be still

I was on vacation in Florida last year with a few of my friends and we decided to spend the day beside a lake. I was sixteen years old at the time. While my friends decided to sit at a picnic table and have a cold drink I decided to go for a swim. It was so very hot. It was stupid and dangerous, but I was young and I thought I would live for ever. I was sure that there wouldn't be any nasties in the water and, besides, I was a strong swimmer.

I got undressed and walked into the lake. It was so refreshing. I walked out a little further and was just about to start swimming when I hit a drop-off and went completely underwater. At first I tried to get back to the surface, but it soon became clear that the current was too strong. I kept on struggling until a voice in my head told me, clearly and firmly, to 'be still'. In a heartbeat I became calm and still and felt myself gently sinking to the bottom of the lake. As I floated down completely still, I felt things brushing against me, things with scales on them, but I have no idea what they were as I could hardly see anything.

When I hit the bottom of the lake, I heard the voice speak to me again and it told me to turn and walk. I didn't think I could move but the voice got louder and I found myself turning to my left and then walking along the bottom of the lake. I walked about a dozen steps and as I did it felt like there was a door in my head slowly closing. Then my head surfaced above the water and I started to panic and struggle again. I also saw my friends on the shore jumping up and down and running into the water to rescue me.

When I got to the shore my friends put me on my stomach and I coughed up what seemed like a gallon of water; it just kept flowing out of me. The next day I called my mum to tell her what had happened. I didn't dare tell any of my friends because I knew they would not have believed me, but I knew that my mum would. When I told her about the voice she asked me what it had sounded like and I said that it was a voice I had not heard before but it was very loud, authoritative and bossy. My mum gasped and told me that she thought it was my grandmother; she had been a schoolteacher, both loved and feared because she was a strict disciplinarian. My grandmother had died when I was five so I don't really have any clear memories of her, but after that incident I feel closer to her than ever. I'm leaving university next year and although I used to have no idea what I wanted to do with my life, I have a clear idea now. I want to do what my grandmother did. I want to teach, and to be as respected as she was by her pupils.

What did Trisha hear when she was under the water? Was it random words spoken by her friends who were probably searching for her on the shore, which she interpreted as a warning to turn around? Or perhaps it was just the instinct of an experienced swimmer? Or was it what Trisha believes it to have been – the voice of an angel? You'd have a struggle convincing Trisha that the specific life-saving and authoritative directions she heard were anything other than a warning from some level of existence with sight reaching further than any of us can imagine.

A calm and authoritative voice from beyond also features in this next story from Heidi:

The co-pilot

I always used to think that people who heard voices were mad or sad, but I don't think I am either of those things. I'm a sane, happy mum of three and I've never in my life heard voices inside my head, until the night of 21 March 2002. This is what happened.

I'd been involved in a minor car crash that day. I didn't have any broken bones but I was fairly shaken up and had been unconscious for a few minutes at the scene so doctors decided to keep me in for observation overnight. I wasn't very happy about it as I hated being away from my family. After they had left my bedside I tried to get to sleep as fast as I could because if I slept morning would come quicker and I could get home. It took a while, as I was a bit sore and whip-lashed, but eventually I did fall asleep. I remember dreaming of a huge aeroplane and I was the pilot. While I was in my dream plane my co-pilot, a young man with the most beautiful blue-green eyes I have ever seen, kept looking at me and telling me to 'wake up'. In my dream I told him I was wide awake but he told me it really was time for me to 'wake up, now, really wake up'.

I didn't want to wake up but I found myself in that twilight zone where you are half asleep and half awake. I kept hearing that voice telling me to wake up, but I was so tired I tried to fight it. The voice, however, was more determined than I was. It wasn't an angry voice, just a very calm and controlled one, and I knew it wasn't going to stop until I did what it asked so I reluctantly forced my eyes open. When I did I saw that the sheets and blankets on my bed were stained red. It shocked me and I cried out. A nurse came running over to me and then several doctors came to my bedside. Before long a whole team were urging me to stay awake as I fought against the over-whelming urge to sleep.

Mercifully, the bleeding stopped and I survived but I don't think I would be writing to you today if the guardian angel in my dream hadn't told me to wake up. It had to be my guardian angel, don't you think?

I wrote back to tell Heidi that, in my opinion, it was her guardian angel appearing to her in the guise of a dream co-pilot. I also told her that her dream of flying in her own plane was a sign that from that moment on her life would never feel the same. She wrote back to tell me she could not agree more. After an angel saved her she decided she had so much more she wanted to do with her life. Having left school with no qualifications she decided to go back to college and she has now set up her own retail business, which is thriving. She told me that it clearly wasn't her time to go and, having been so close to death, she was determined to make every day count.

These next two stories fit perfectly here because, although they are both unique, they do share certain similarities with Heidi's 'waking up' theme. The first was sent to me by Grace:

The open door

It was the middle of the night and my little girl, Tana, came running into my bedroom to tell me someone had woken her up by opening and shutting her bedroom door. Now, there was no one in the house except me and her but she seemed really unsettled so I let her snuggle under the bedclothes with me. In a few moments we were both fast asleep again but this time it was me who woke up and noticed my bedroom door open very slowly and then shut very slowly again. It was weird to say the least but I thought it must be a draft so I drifted back off to sleep. Next thing I knew I heard a voice tell me to get up. I don't know why, but I instinctively obeyed. When I opened my bedroom door I noticed immediately that there was smoke all over the house.

To cut a long story short, a fire had started in my kitchen. I'd left a pan on the stove. I grabbed my little girl and ran out of the house as fast as I could.

I believe an angel opened and closed our bedroom door that night and when I refused to pay attention I believe an angel spoke to me. My house was destroyed and I lost some treasured items but I gained something far more precious: the knowledge that my angel was watching over me and my little girl.

This next story from Jo is absorbing because it shows that we often don't know what is in our best interests, and even if we do hear the voice of an angel we often do our best to ignore it.

Get out of my seat

I always thought if I was going to hear the voice of my guardian angel it would sound sweet and be accompanied by a chorus of beautiful singing and sweet harp music. I had no idea it would sound just like the voice of an exasperated schoolmistress.

I was at a local council meeting, feeling rather bored as the topic did not interest me. I was sitting on my own wondering what on earth I was doing there when I heard a voice say, 'Get out of my seat.' It was so sharp and clear I turned around to see who this rather rude person was, as nobody had a claim on any of the seats, but there was no one there. So I decided to ignore it, but a few seconds later there it was again. This time, though, it was even louder. I looked around but again there was nobody there. I even looked up at the ceiling to see if anybody was sitting on a window-sill or something and trying to get my attention.

By now the meeting was in full swing, although there were only about four or five of us in the audience. I tried to listen – but this voice just kept on interrupting. Eventually, I felt so hassled by it that I got up and moved several seats away. About ten minutes later, a brick came hurtling through the window, shattering it and landing right where I would have been sitting. It was the scariest but also the most wonderful moment of my life. I had moved out of the way in time. If I had sat there for minutes longer I would have been seriously injured for sure, or even worse.

Even though I did all I could to ignore it, an angel saved me that day. How wonderful, how amazing is that?

You can just sense Jo's excitement in the way she tells her story. I love her story also because it underlines the fact that as far as our angels are concerned it really is important to let go of preconceived notions of what they may or may not look or sound like. They have this habit of surprising us and manifesting in ways we least expect.

When I read them I just knew I had to include this next

cluster of angel-saved-me stories in this book – all of them extraordinary in their own way. I hope you feel as excited and enthused reading them as I did when they were first sent to me. Remember that calm voice from beyond that I mentioned earlier? It appears again in Lily's story below.

In at the deep end

Twenty years ago when my son Ben was eighteen months old we went with a couple of my mum friends and their kids to our local swimming pool. It was the first time swimming for my Ben and I was very excited. The other mums had all been taking their children to the pool for quite some time, but they assured me they would look after us.

As often happens when you get a group of mums and toddlers out together, there were loads of distractions. I told Ben to sit quietly while I blew up his armbands but before I knew it he was running away in a frenzy of excitement. My knees have always been very weak so I found it hard to keep up with him and in a trice he was on the other side of the pool, by the deep end, waving at me. I started to make my way around to him. I didn't panic at this stage because he was a fairly timid boy, and I thought he would stay away from the water, but as soon as he saw his friends splashing around with their mums in the shallow end he decided he was going to join in. My heart stood still when I saw him jump in.

It took me a moment to get to him. I cried out for help but the pool was so noisy I don't think anybody heard me and the lifeguard must have gone out for something because there was no one sitting in the high chair. I knew that I had to jump in and save Ben, but I couldn't swim very well myself. I was just about to jump in when I heard a clear, cool voice say in my right ear, 'You can save him from here.' I threw myself down on my knees and leaned into the water. I reached down until my face was under the water and I saw Ben's hair floating up towards me. I grabbed his hair and pulled him up. It must have hurt him quite a bit because when I got him out of the water he was screaming and spluttering. To me it was the most beautiful sound in the world.

I looked around me but there was nobody close by. The voice I had heard wasn't my own. It definitely belonged to someone else but I have no idea who or what spoke to me. It's something that has intrigued me for the last twenty years until my sister started to talk to me about angels and I read one of your books. I truly believe an angel spoke to me that day.

And by the way, after that incident I enrolled Ben on a proper swimming course and he went on to compete for his school at national level. I'm still afraid of the water and prefer to stay at the shallow end of swimming pools, but I shall never forget the miracle that happened to me when I did venture over to the deep end.

In this next story, sent to me by Cordelia, there appears to be a full-blown angel sighting.

Collision

I was walking to the shops with my three children, getting ready to cross the road, when I witnessed a violent collision right in front of my eyes. It involved a truck and a Mercedes. The Mercedes did a complete 360-degree spin in the air before heading into another oncoming car and rolling up its bonnet. I feared for the people inside that car as the Merc was sure to shatter their windscreen and maybe even continue rolling over them, but it didn't. At that moment the Merc just stopped in mid-air and rolled slowly back onto the road. It was crazy. The Merc was travelling at such speed – how on earth did it just stop like that? My son standing next to me described it well when he said that it looked like it was a remote control car and someone just pushed a button to change its direction.

Mercifully, nobody was badly hurt in the collision. The driver of the Merc had a few cuts and bruises and the truck was seriously damaged but its driver also escaped unhurt. As for the car that nearly got rolled over, it was driven by a middle-aged woman who was taking her dog to the vet. She got out of the car looking dazed but again no injuries. Her dog was just fine too. There must have been a lot of angels flying around that day!

If that wasn't miracle enough, when my kids and I were finally able to get on our way my youngest daughter, aged six, looked at me and asked me if I had seen the angels. I told her I hadn't but she told me she had seen two angels sitting on the bonnet of the car that was nearly rolled over. When the Merc had approached they stood up, held out their hands and stopped the car in mid-air before gently setting it down. I asked her what the angels looked like and she just said, 'Angels.' I tried to get more details but she wouldn't give me any. The question I want to ask you is: did my daughter really see something or has she just got an overactive imagination?

We'll talk more about children and angels in chapter seven, but for now I think you know my answer: I believe lots of angels were on duty for Cordelia and her children that day. Holly also believes she saw an angel. Here's what she told me.

I saw an angel

Another driver struck my car head on. A split second before impact I saw my guardian angel standing directly in front of my car. She was yellow. She had yellow hair, yellow eyes and yellow skin and an enormous pair of yellow wings. I had my brother in the back of the car and he thought I was about to hit a pedestrian. He said she looked just like an ordinary woman, but that's impossible because we were on a motorway. He didn't see any yellow.

To cut an endless story short my only injury was a cut to my forehead and my brother had a knee injury. I don't get the significance of the colour yellow as I'm a Goth and wear mostly black, so I don't know why my guardian angel is yellow, but I'm in awe and deeply humbled to have been saved in this way. I feel so lucky to be alive.

Nicky sent me this simple but charming little story. She didn't see an angel but she believes her friend's daughter did.

Smells like rain

My friend told me this story. I believe it one hundred per cent because she is the kindest, most honest and true person I know. Eight years ago she gave birth to a premature baby boy. Her son was so frail and small it was highly unlikely he would survive more than a few days. He was put in an incubator in the premature baby unit and his parents sat by him day and night praying for him to live. They talked to him, stroked him and held his little fingers.

The little boy defied the predictions of the doctors and the days he was expected to survive turned into weeks and the weeks into months. Everybody was astonished at the fighting spirit he showed. After four months he was no longer considered high risk and was thriving. It was a miracle.

Fast-forward five years and this little boy is playing football in the garden with his dad. It started to rain and his dad picked him up to take him indoors. The little boy then said something incredible. He told his dad that this is what 'he' smelled like. The dad asked him what he was talking about and the little boy replied, 'You know, him. When I was littler I slept on his chest and he hugged me and kept me warm.'

The dad knew what his son was talking about. He was talking about his guardian angel, the angel who kept him safe when he was a tiny baby and his life hung in the balance.

And I'd like to round things off here with this marvellous rescue story sent to me by Joan, because it features two kinds of angels – the human and the divine.

Up in flames

Fifteen years ago my sister's house went up in flames. She managed to get out with two of her children, but her daughter, who was six at the time, and her newborn baby son were still inside. Firefighters had arrived on the scene in record time and were battling to control the blaze. Some of them ran inside the house with hoses and others stayed outside to direct water onto the flames. Inside the house it was hard to see because the smoke was so thick, but they managed to get to the nursery and rescue the baby. Time was running out, though, for my little niece.

By now the house was burning hot and a frightening place to be. My sister had to be restrained because I know she would have climbed back in to save her daughter if she had been allowed. It would have been perfectly understandable if the firemen had decided it was too dangerous to re-enter, but they didn't hesitate and two of them went right back in. One of them had to admit defeat and came back out minutes later. He was struggling to breathe. The second, though, didn't come back. Instead he crawled around on what was left of the living-room floor until he felt someone's leg. When he touched it the girl cried out. He gave her some oxygen before tucking her under his arms.

By now the fireman was disorientated. He knew he had to get out but could not see anything. He had no idea which direction would take him to safety. It was then that he saw what looked like another child standing beside the burning staircase. At first he panicked, thinking it was another child that needed saving, but then he realised it was something otherworldly. This child had flames in her hair, but her dress was not burning and she was smiling and pointing. She wasn't crying out or screaming, she was just pointing. He knew he had to follow her directions and he soon realised she was pointing to a door, a door that would lead them safely outside. When he got to the door he turned around but there was no sign of the child that had saved them both. She had vanished. It was only later when the fireman told my sister this story that he – and she and everyone else, including me, who heard his story – knew for sure that this brave man had seen his guardian angel.

You may have noticed in most of the heavenly rescue stories you've read so far that the term guardian angel is often used, but what exactly is your guardian angel? I hope the following explanation will be enlightening.

Your guardian angel

Guardian angels are said to be personally assigned to each one of us at conception – or before if you believe in reincarnation – regardless of faith, character or lifestyle, to guide us and protect us from harm, and they stay with us throughout our entire lives and beyond. Your guardian angel is unique to you and will walk with you wherever you go and whatever you do. They have never lived as humans on earth, although they may take on human form briefly as 'incarnated angels'. Whether there is one guardian angel per person, or several angels for one person, is open to question and a matter of personal belief.

Guardian angels are manifestations of pure love and they bring to us only what will help us, guide us, protect us and encourage us to aspire to the greatest potential of our soul. They can bring us rays of light during times of darkness. If we make choices that do not bring us closer to the light they can't interfere with our free will but they can show us how to make more positive choices.

Sometimes your guardian angel reveals itself through a full-blown angel encounter, complete with wings and halo, but, as you've already seen, it is far more likely to come in subtler, gentler ways, such as inspiring us with a thought that prompts us to take positive action. Sometimes we are are lent superhuman strength, or sent a premonition that guides us to safety or averts potential disaster. In fact, there are many instances that are often put down to luck, coincidence or even a miracle, but which have the touch of a hand of light behind them. On other occasions, there may be an unexpected feeling of warmth or comfort, or in times of sadness or grief it may feel as if an invisible cloak of feathered wings is wrapping itself softly around you. For others, an inexplicable presence is felt − like a sudden rush of air created by the passing of an 'angel on a mission' at the speed of light, or there may be the feeling of an invisible kiss, or the sense that someone is standing close behind you. Sometimes other people will offer you hugs and comfort. I always know that my guardian angel is close by when my children are particularly affectionate. Never discount the idea that your guardian angel can use other people to bring its message of love and comfort. Your angel will use whatever means it can to touch your heart.

In this next story Melanie talks about some of the gentle ways in which her guardian angel reassures her.

Wonderful signs

After I lost custody of my small sons I fell apart. It was a miscarriage of justice and I was filled with heartache and feelings of isolation.

One night, I was in bed crying for hours. I was so eaten alive by grief I thought I was going to die of a broken heart. Suddenly, I felt unseen hands gently stroking the top of my back to comfort me. There was no fear – I sensed they were angels who knew my situation. I was totally comforted by their angelic presence and stopped weeping.

My sons are now young adults and I am still working hard to mend the damage that was done to the bond between us. About two years ago, my youngest was angry about changes going on in his dad's life and for no reason and with no explanation he cut me out of his life for eighteen long months. Once again my heart was broken and the old wounds reopened. I wrote to him and sent him countless texts. I never gave up on him and not once did I stop praying for help. I sensed his distress and it was torture not to be about to comfort him directly.

One Saturday evening I had a bath and then went to my bedroom to dry off. The room was in darkness and I was feeling quite overheated so I decided to lie down on the floor to cool down. There I lay, relaxing in the dark of the room when I saw what looked like a star made of gold light flash briefly in the air in front of me. Then a second one did the same thing. I was astonished and thought at first I needed to see an optician, but later I realised that it was a spiritual sign, not my eyes.

The next day, my mobile rang and it was my son phoning to break the long silence. Neither of us mentioned the gap in contact but I was overjoyed to hear his voice again. My intuition tells me that the 'gold stars' shown to me were a piece of heaven sent to tell me of the happy news about to unfold the next day. It was a wonderful sign!

Then there are times when for no reason at all you get a feeling of being loved and connected to everyone and everything. Or perhaps you experience a deep sense of release concerning something that has been worrying or stressing you out. You let go of your worries and suddenly everything falls into place. Again this is your guardian angel at work helping you to trust and let go, so that heaven can intervene on your behalf. Your guardian angel may manifest most strongly in times of danger or when you are at a low or desperate point in your life and in urgent need of spiritual support. This has certainly been the case for me. In all my angel books, you'll find mention of the many times my guardian angel has quite literally saved my life and, of course, you'll read stories from other people who feel the same way. The deeper – or should that be higher – meaning of all this is that even when we feel we have failed, we can't cope or are at our lowest, our guardian angel is still right beside us.

We all get moments of darkness when we feel that our lives have no purpose. I certainly get my fair share of them, but whereas in the past I might have felt depressed and confused, I now think about all the twists and turns of my life that have brought me to the place I am today, all the dark times my guardian angel has stood right beside me. This helps me see that I'm alive today because my guardian knows that I still have a purpose here on earth and, as you are reading this now, so do you. There is something that only you can do.

Never lose sight of the fact that your life has meaning and purpose. It is more precious than you may ever know and there will come a time when you can see your light and value. You will see yourself as your guardian angel has always seen you. Your guardian angel longs for you to see yourself in this way now. You are not meant to feel confused and depressed and alone. These are just emotions fear has taught you during those times when you were not connected to your angels and did not know that the universe is powered by joy, hope and love.

So, the next time you feel confused or depressed and unsure, ask your guardian angel for joy, love and hope. Ask for comfort and courage and faith. All this and more is yours for the taking in every moment and all of it can turn your life around in a heartbeat. This is your guardian angel's purpose: to help you live in the light and help you understand that when you pray for good things the universe moves towards you. All your guardian angel requires you to do is to ask for these things with a sense of gratitude, as if you already have them, because this shows you have faith and an open heart.

Some people believe that your guardian angel is actually your higher self, or the divine spark within you, but whether you discover your guardian angel within or around you, the impact on your spiritual transformation is one and the same. In much the same way, whether you believe in angels or not, your guardian angel is always by your side, but the more faith you have in your guardian angel's presence the stronger the connection will be. My advice then would be to treat your guardian angel just as you would your dearest, most loving friend. Nurture your relationship with them, take hold of their hands and let them lead you out of the darkness. Remember that when you take a little step of faith towards them, they take several leaps towards you!

And while we are on the subject of faith, I'm going to complete this chapter with a story that speaks volumes about its life-saving. It's a pretty well-known story, but it is so incredible I'm sure you won't mind revisiting it.

We never lost faith

In August 2010, thirty-three men were trapped in a Chilean mine for more than two months. After an incredible rescue all the men emerged unharmed and healthy. Although the Chilean government spared no expense or effort to rescue them, one has to ask if their survival in the harshest of conditions was a miracle. For the rescued miners, there was no doubt in their minds: it was a miracle, or a series of miracles. First, the men were not killed when the mine collapsed, second they were all saved, and third a miracle of human skill, ingenuity and strength brought them back to the surface.

While underground the men found comfort and hope in their prayers. Miner Mario Sepulveda described their sentiments: 'We never lost faith. We knew we would be rescued.' Sepulveda, the second miner to be freed, said, 'I have been with God and I've been with the devil . . . I seized the hand of God. I always knew God would get us out of there.'

Doctors and psychologists were surprised by the excellent condition of the men when they emerged from the mine, considering the high levels of stress they had been under. All had tolerated the harrowing ordeal in a truly exceptional way and no serious psychological or physical problems were found. It was a real miracle and doctors and psychologists were hard pressed to explain the healthy condition of the men. The miners and their loved ones, who were sustained by their spirituality, however, were less surprised as they attributed their happy ending to their faith.

We all need to be rescued sometimes.

Of course, the Chilean mine rescue was a fantastic story showcasing the best of humanity and the true power of faith, but its significance has, in my opinion, a lot more to do with the engagement of so many people on a spiritual level. Few of us were unmoved by the miners' plight and all were elated when they were rescued, but our fascination with the miners and sympathy for their imprisonment was so all-consuming because it tapped into our own, often unexpressed spiritual need for purpose and meaning in our lives. In other words, the story of the miners in Chile may have consciously or unconsciously had many people all over the world wondering what their own lives were about. It reminded us that we all need to see the light at the end of the tunnel; we all need to be rescued sometimes.

If you are reading this book and wondering what your life is all about, and whether there is anyone out there who will rescue you, I hope you will begin to see that each one of us has a divine meaning and purpose and that our angels can help us get in touch with this meaning and purpose. I hope you will be reminded that whoever you are and however tough, unfair, trivial, dark or painful your life feels, you are never alone; your guardian angel is always there to guide you. I hope you will recognise that you are important and that your contribution to the world by your words, actions, thoughts and prayers is also important, because it can bring light and healing to yourself and to others, and by so doing make the world a better and brighter place.

The miners were rescued and in a sense we can all be rescued. All we need to do is believe ... truly believe.

CHAPTER FOUR

Awakenings

Of course you don't die. Nobody dies. Death doesn't exist. You only reach a new level of vision, a new realm of consciousness, a new unknown world.

Henry Miller

According to near-death accounts, the reason for our very existence is to attain spiritual growth. We are more of a spiritual being than we are a physical being.

Kevin Williams

Perhaps no 'angel saved my life' stories are as compelling as those that involve near-death experiences. Near-death experiences are common enough to have entered our everyday language. Phrases like 'My whole life flashed before my eyes,' and 'Go into the light' come from decades of research into these often reported supernatural experiences. But what is it that people see and feel as they stand on the brink of life? And do their experiences offer any solid evidence of an afterlife?

Even though I have not had one myself, for as long as I can remember near-death experiences have fascinated me, and I think I have devoured almost every book and study ever written on the subject. For the purposes of this book, a near-death experience is any experience in which someone close to death or suffering from some trauma, illness or intense emotional crisis perceives events that seem to be impossible or supernatural. While there are many questions about near-death experiences, one thing is certain — they do exist. Thousands of people have perceived similar sensations while close to death.

The term near-death experience, abbreviated to NDE, was coined by Dr Raymond Moody in his 1975 book *Life After Life*, although reports of such experiences have been recorded throughout history, beginning with Plato's account of a soldier named Er who was apparently killed in battle. Fortunately for Er, he revived on the funeral pyre and stated that while unconscious he had left his body and travelled to a strange place where he had seen other dead soldiers choosing their next life.

Due to advances in modern medicine and research, especially in resuscitation techniques, reports of near-death experiences have been very widespread in recent years, with studies showing that as many as 43 per cent of people who have been clinically dead and then revived have had the experience. Prior religious or spiritual belief or knowledge of NDEs does *not* increase the likelihood of experiencing one. Every NDE is unique but there are also certain similarities. Typically, there is an overwhelming sense of peace and acceptance followed by a brilliant white light. The person may feel disconnected from their body in some way. They may look down on it and see doctors working on it. Then they may find themselves following the light into a tunnel. In that tunnel they may meet angels or the spirits of loved ones or see their entire life in flashback. Sometimes they may hear a voice telling them that it is not their time and they need to go back.

Of course, scientists, doctors and experts have put forward many theories to explain NDEs, but none of their theories can explain away the strong similarities that tend to occur in NDEs regardless of a person's culture, background and circumstances. The research that really fascinated me most, though, wasn't that which presented theories for whether NDEs are supernatural experiences or not, but the research on the effect an NDE has on a person's life.

Kenneth King, one of the most respected and widely read researchers of NDE stories, reports that a large number of people gain more self-belief after such an experience. There is a significant and positive change in their attitude towards life. This typically includes a sense of purpose, an appreciation of life, an increase in compassion, patience and understanding and an overall feeling of personal strength. Most significant of all is that NDE subjects tend to feel a heightened sense of spirituality, but this does not mean they turn towards religion or church attendance – it is more of an internal and personal spiritual connection that fills them with a sense of wholeness or well-being that may have been lacking before. And last, but by no means least, they often say that they no longer fear death and believe that a positive experience awaits them on the other side.

For me, King's research silences any doubts I might have had about the validity of NDEs, because if an experience brings a person closer to the world of spirit, or changes their lives in a positive way, the source is divine. It is a life-saving heavenly encounter. I could talk endlessly about NDEs, but it doesn't really matter what I think or believe about them — what really matters is what *you* think or believe. If you aren't sure, I hope the following stories will help you make up your mind or enlighten, inform or move you in some way. Reading about what people have actually seen, felt or learned during a near-death experience can be hugely beneficial. It can encourage thoughtful living and be a source of hope and comfort by raising the very real possibility that life does not end with death. Jacky's story is a fine place to start.

I'm ready

Let me tell you about the day I died. It happened in 1993. I was a schoolteacher and mother of four children and passionate about the environment. I guess I was a bit ahead of my time because back then it certainly wasn't the burning issue in the media that it is today. Before I died I wasn't what you would call spiritual. I believed in our being kind to one another, and in treating as you would be treated, but that was about it. I had no idea what happened to us after death and the rational part of me assumed that we simply become worm food.

On the day I died I remember feeling extremely stressed. My youngest daughter was down with a heavy cold and it was getting close to examination time at school for my pupils and I really didn't want to take a day off. After a lot of begging and pleading I got my sister to come round with her two children – she was a stay-at-home mum back then – and she agreed to help me out for the day. By the time I had sorted all that out I was a good hour late for school so I really put my foot down when I was finally able to get in my car and drive to the school.

What happened next was utterly mind-blowing. I was driving towards a set of traffic lights. I saw them turn amber but decided to go for it. It was a stupid, stupid thing to do because I hit another car head-on. I heard noise, grinding metal and then everything went black. The next thing I remember is opening my eyes in a hospital bed and a team of medical workers barking orders at each other. Then I felt my eyelids get very heavy and as they did I knew I was going to die. I fell into the blackness again.

Next thing I remember is standing beside my body watching the doctors working on it. I was fully aware. I could see myself and the medical team but not the room I was in – I was standing in blackness. It didn't scare me, though. I was just happy to be there. I wanted to stay with my body, but then I felt this bright light shining on me. I had this irresistible urge to step into the light. It was pulling me towards it like a magnet.

I turned away from my body and started to move towards the light. It was the most beautiful thing I have ever seen. It was like all the comfort, love and happiness you have ever craved in your life moving towards you. I wanted to merge with it. I knew then that the sole purpose of life is to love and what distorts people is life without love. I wanted to become a part of the light. I said, 'I'm ready.'

Suddenly, I was pulled up into the stream of light. I floated in it like a feather. It was warm and intoxicating. The truth became obvious to me. There is no death. I was limited but also endless and spirit infused every part of my being, just as it infused every blade of grass and every atom of creation. I saw everything as spirit and light. I saw everything as alive.

At that point I just knew I was going back to my body. I was a human again. I wasn't told — I just knew. But from what I had experienced I would have been happy to come back as an ant in our universe or even a pebble on the beach. All aspects of creation are a living miracle. Every person, no matter how conflicted, is a blessing and everything, no matter how apparently trivial, is a blessing also.

Even though I knew I was going back, it was strange to find myself opening my eyes again back in my body. I could feel electric shocks going through my body and hands pumping my chest. I could hear the medical team cheering and a doctor saying, 'She's back.' Apparently I had died for seven minutes.

For the next few hours I did not recall what I had experienced. I kept waking up and falling asleep again, unsure if I was dreaming, dead or alive. I still had no memory of it a few days later but then my memory was triggered when my doctor told me in more detail what had happened. I listened but my ears and my heart really opened wide when I heard him tell me that just before I died, my final words were 'I'm ready.'

It was at that moment that my memories came flooding back. I remembered with absolute clarity what I had experienced. I told my doctor and he listened with interest. He said that he had heard similar stories from other patients hovering close to death and it wasn't his place to pass judgement on whether it was real or not. But I know what I experienced was real because since the day I died I have found absolutely nothing wrong with any human being. I can't judge people any more. I also stress far less about environmental issues because I now know that problems like this can bring us together and anything that brings us together is a blessing. And I also know beyond any doubt that death really is nothing at all. Since this time, I've never had a fear of dying. Like most near-death experiencers, I know there is something more after we leave our body. I don't know what it is, but you don't die, you just leave the body's 'shell'.

I realised that I didn't need to die to come to this peaceful and contented place. It was always there inside me waiting for the moment when I said, 'I'm ready.'

Luke's story is another good example of how an NDE can be a source of hope, comfort and encouragement, and not just to the person directly involved, but to others as well.

Turn around

I had a NDE in 2004 when I was twenty-two and I was clinically dead from septicaemia. I knew that I had died because my body didn't feel like it fitted me any more, or belonged to me. The most stunning thing was that I felt more alive in the light – or when I was so-called 'dead'– than when I was on earth. I found myself living in this light and there were more colours there than I have ever seen. I didn't see angels or a tunnel or old friends. I was alone, but completely unafraid and at peace. I've heard others describe the warm feeling of being back in the womb – this is close. You feel warm, weightless and safe, without a care in the world. I was happy to be there, intensely happy, and I really wanted to stay, but then I felt myself turning around and I was shown an image of myself helping children to read and write. It knew it was time for me to go back and I snapped back into my body.

My experience was quite literally life-changing. Inspired by my vision I left business school and went to train as a primary school teacher. I'm now fully qualified and have worked in several schools, both in this country and abroad. I don't get paid much but I get something much more important than money. I know that I am having an impact on young lives. It is wonderful to see children learn and improve but I don't just teach them the facts; I try to teach them to believe in themselves and to trust that their lives have meaning.

NDEs typically occur when a person is close to death or in danger of losing their life, but in some rare instances this isn't necessarily the case, as Isabelle's story illustrates:

Hold my hand

I'm a middle-aged woman and sometimes I treat myself to an afternoon nap. Last month I had an astonishing experience and I knew I had to write and tell you about it. I fell asleep and found myself leaving my body. It was as if someone invisible took my hand and gently pulled me out. Then I felt myself being led out of my living room and out of my house. I didn't walk, I floated, and I floated several streets away from my house. I passed people by and I'm sure one or two of them saw me because I saw them look up or turn around and smile at me. Then I came to a junction and I saw an ambulance at the scene of a crash. I could see that a car had smashed into a wall and that a woman was trapped under the car.

I felt myself floating towards the car and then I reached my hand into it. The car just seemed to melt away at my touch. I saw a woman lying on the ground looking dazed and scared. I held out my hand to her and she smiled and reached out to me. Now it was my turn to lead her and I found myself taking her high up into the sky. For a brief instant we were connected. It was as if we were the same person and then I felt myself leading her towards a ball of light. It was so warm and inviting and we both glided towards it. Once inside I felt the awesome power of love in every part of my being. I wanted to go further but the light only let the woman travel on. I found myself turning around and floating back to my house. As I did I saw the woman's body being taken out from under the car and a group of paramedics administering first aid. I don't remember any more because the next thing I knew I was waking up because my phone was ringing.

At the time I thought I had had a strange dream, but a week later I found myself at the junction I had visited in my dream. I saw several bunches of flowers in the spot where I had witnessed the car crash. I made some enquiries and found out that there had indeed been a crash a week previously, and a woman had died. There was a photograph of her in the local newspaper and I recognised her instantly.

I believe I helped that woman cross over to the other side. I also believe I was given a privileged glimpse of life on the other side. It was truly awesome and I feel truly blessed. It has changed everything in my life. For a start, I don't take naps any more. I am far too busy living. I've also signed up for a degree course starting in September. It's always been a dream of mine to have letters after my name. I've got back in touch with my mum, after years of silence following a family feud, and last, but by no means least, I hope to train as a bereavement counsellor one day. I'd like to help people lose their fear of death, both when I am awake and when I fall asleep.

This story probably falls into the category of an out-of-body experience or OBE, which we will look at in more detail in the next chapter. There can be a certain amount of crossover between an NDE and an OBE, but for now I'd like to draw your attention to something Isabelle stresses in her story, and it's something the great majority of people who have had an NDE also report, and this is that the experience was a turning point in their lives.

Brian, who relates his story below, also felt that his NDR was a blessing in disguise.

The right track

I was quite literally heading down the wrong track when I had my NDE two years ago. I had this deep-seated anger at everyone, including myself, and my life was consumed with the desire for power and possessions. I had two broken marriages behind me because I was verbally and on the odd occasion physically abusive to women. I wouldn't admit it to myself but I also had a drinking problem and I was way over the limit when I crashed my car. I died for forty-five minutes that day as medics battled to save me. There was another person involved in the crash – a young girl – and she was seriously injured and still limps badly to this day.

You may not want to read on now – and I don't blame you. I am fully aware of the heartache and pain, both physical and emotional, I have caused others, and it is a source of deep regret to me. I do hope, though, that if you do decide to read on, what you read will make sense to you, as it does to me.

After the crash I was barely conscious. I remember seeing my clothes soaked in my own blood as my head had been split open. I remember the paramedics talking to each other and then I slipped into unconsciousness. I use the word unconsciousness because it is the only way I can describe it. In reality I could see my body in the ambulance and then I was whisked away from the ambulance at the speed of light. I saw loads of lights around me and then I was confronted by this huge white tunnel. I was sucked into the tunnel.

Apologies if all this sounds really odd. I assure you I am not still drinking, but when I was in that tunnel for the first time in my life I felt no anger, no fear. I did not worry about what might happen to me. I felt so light. It was a lovely, enchanting and liberating experience. It was a state of pure bliss.

All too soon I felt my spirit rushing away at great speed. I was back in the ambulance and I saw myself step back into my body. I opened my eyes and felt incredibly sad to leave all that love and peace behind and then the most horrible thing happened. I felt all my anger and my self-absorption shock back into me. It was unbearable. I felt violated. I didn't want to be brought back like that.

For the next two days my life hung in the balance but eventually I pulled through. I was told that I had no permanent brain damage. Since then doctors have tried to tell me that my experience was an hallucination but I know better than that. I was more real in that ambulance than I had been all of my life. Now, instead of chasing women, power and money, I search for that lightness, that liberty of spirit I felt on the day I nearly died. I don't want to be weighed down by anger, jealousy and greed any more. It is an unbearable existence.

I have no idea why I survived that day – I certainly didn't deserve to – but I am determined to turn my life around. I haven't touched a drop of alcohol since. I have given a large cash settlement to the young girl I injured. She refuses to see me, and I know money can never undo what I did, but I hope it will help her in some small way. And finally, I am determined to fill the black hole inside me with love because I know that when my time comes that is how I will be judged – not by what I have accomplished, but by how I have loved.

I truly and wholeheartedly believe that reading about NDEs can help change our attitude to life. It can show that every one of us, however undeserving we may feel, is here for a purpose and that purpose is to love. It can also show us that death is a wonderful new beginning. It is natural to fear death, and losing a loved one can be one of life's most distressing experiences. If, however, we can understand that death is nothing to be afraid of, it can help us live our lives as we were meant to – to the full.

There could be no better place than now to put this next story sent to me by Will fifteen years ago. Sadly, Will died recently but his spirit and this remarkable story live on.

Timeless

When I was fifty-six I had a near-death experience. It changed my life.

On the day I died I was recovering from a bout of flu. I was still very weak but I've always hated being ill and couldn't resist popping down to the gym for a few hours. Being fit and keeping my body beautiful were always very important to me. I tried to sweat out the last of the infection but instead I ended up collapsing. I remember getting out of the shower after my workout and feeling very light-headed before suddenly feeling violent stabbing pains in my heart, chest and arms.

Suddenly all the pain melted away, I felt weightless and began gently to float up and out of my body, which was lying on the chang-ing-room floor. This didn't upset me; in fact quite the opposite – I was very happy to know I wasn't going back to my body. I looked around and saw a beautiful white light down a long tunnel. I knew I was going to head down it and a familiar, comforting sensation spun around and inside me. I was going home. I began to spin faster into this gorgeous light. I came to the light and was immediately surrounded by angels. I recognised each and every one of them and realised how much I had missed them.

Then I started watching my life. It is hard to describe but I was watching it yet I was part of it at the same time. I saw everything I had ever said and done and I saw how my words, thoughts and actions had impacted others. I saw how many times I had made others laugh and how many times I had made them cry. It hurt me deeply when I saw the suffering I had caused others, but then I saw the times when

116

love had flowed freely from me to others. I also saw them turn around and spread my love to others.

Then I was told – and the voice that spoke sounded as if it was mine – that it was time for me to return to my body. There was still more work for me to do. I felt incredible sadness and when I jolted back into my body the feelings of heaviness and pain were hard to bear. I had tasted such freedom.

The gym phoned for an ambulance and within half an hour I was lying in a hospital bed recovering. After a series of tests I was told that I had had a stroke and from now on I needed to be really careful. I needed to make sure I didn't put my body under a great deal of stress. I was also told that I might not regain full use of the right side of my body.

If I had not had my near-death experience being virtually a cripple would have devastated me. My life up until that point had been about sports and fitness – I was a personal trainer – and exercise was my overriding passion in life; but quite literally in a heartbeat all that was taken away from me and I had to reinvent myself. It hasn't been a problem, though, because I know that I am far more than my physical being. I am a spiritual being with a body. We are spiritual beings that live for ever. Earth is not our true home, just as my body is not what defines me.

Above all, I no longer fear death. I no longer wonder if there is an afterlife. I think before my experience a lot of my obsession with fitness and appearance was a misguided attempt to feel invincible, like I could live for ever, overcome anything, even death. Many atheists and scientists believe what I experienced is just a trick of the brain, but I disagree. What my NDE gave me was confidence that there is life after death and that we are loved infinitely and eternally. The experience was one of great beauty, freedom and love.

It's been two years since my NDE and I have renewed respect for my life. It's not always been easy and there have been many ups and downs, but I have changed my life for the better. I treat my body with care, and treasure my children and my role as a husband, father and grandfather. Nearly dying has taught me to live my life more deeply and passionately.

It is certainly well documented that one of the most impressive features of NDEs is the profound impact they have on many of those who experience them. Like Will, they often become more spiritual, changing their attitude to their lives and their careers so they can be of service to others, or so they can live their life more deeply. Blind people become sighted for the first time during an NDE, and others tell of finding a sense of purpose and belonging that had eluded them before.

An NDE is without doubt a catalyst for change, a supernatural shock that can save lives and change minds and open hearts to the world of spirit. But you don't need a brush with death to see or hear your angels. Remember, your guardian angel is always right beside you, waiting, hoping and longing for you to look up.

Parting visions

Deathbed or parting visions are closely related to NDEs, the only difference being that the person experiencing the vision does not typically return to life, or have much longer to live. Like NDEs, deathbed visions are far more common than you might think and the traits they display are also surprisingly similar across nationalities, religions and cultures. For instance, people talk of seeing beings of light or spirits of loved ones waiting to escort them over to the other side and the sensation is incredibly reassuring. Above all, the vision has a positive effect on the dying person, moving them from pain and fear to relief from pain and a sense of elation.

Such visions stand alongside NDEs as gripping proof of life after death because, in many cases, the person does not seem to be hallucinating or in an altered state of consciousness because of medication. Wanda's story, below, is a tranquil example.

Gently flying

My husband, Steve, died of cancer on 26 May 2004. It was his wish to die at home so with help from the local hospice he came home a week before he died. We had been married twenty-seven years. There had been tough times, but they were far outweighed by the good and we both knew we were soul mates. I like to think of that last week as a kind of second honeymoon. He was still lucid and we talked for hours about everything, including his death and how we would meet in heaven.

On the day he died Steve said very little. I knew it would not be long before he left me. I sat with him and held his hand. He just lay back and smiled at me. It was a beautiful moment. I did cry, but they were tears of happiness and gratitude for the years we had shared. His breathing started to get heavy and I felt his hand tighten on mine and then he looked at me and said, 'Ma.' I knew then that he was not seeing me any more. He was seeing his mother in spirit. He then looked above my head and it was a look of such otherworldly peace and calmness that I knew an angel was ready to take his spirit home. Then he whispered the word 'flying', closed his eyes and gently died.

It was a beautiful, perfect death for a beautiful, perfect man.

Equally astonishing and moving is Michael's story:

Stay

My mum died at the age of ninety-one. She was admitted to hospital with a broken hip and never fully recovered. I had been told she was frail and that her already poor vision had deteriorated further, but I was not told that she was close to death, so when I went to visit her I was in a fairly relaxed mood. I think she knew, though, because when it was time for me to leave, she held my hand and said, 'Stay.' My mum had always been a very independent, strong-willed lady and it was unusual for her to make a request like this so I asked the nurses if I could stay overnight with her.

That night while my mum slept I sat in a chair reading beside her bed. Suddenly I heard her clear her throat. I looked up and her brown eyes were wide open. She looked to the side of the room and then the ceiling and then she pointed at something above her. I looked up and I saw a butterfly on the ceiling – without her specs on mum was virtually blind, so I have no idea how she saw this. I looked around me to see if I could find a cup or something to catch it and put it outside but when I looked back the butterfly had gone.

Mum smiled at me and I held her hand again. I looked at her and saw all the pain and age disappear from her face. Then she closed her eyes. I thought about getting a nurse to check on her, but with her eyes closed Mum clenched my hand again and said, 'Stay. They're here.' I knew that this was the last time I would be with my mum while she was alive. She looked so beautiful. I bent over and kissed her forehead. She let out a long sigh and I believe that was the moment she passed over. I waited for a few moments before getting the nurses. This was a sacred and precious moment and I never wanted to forget it.

Although deathbed visions have been recorded since the beginning of time, one of the first to subject them to scientific study was Sir William Barrett, a Professor of Physics at the Royal College of Science in Dublin. In his 1926 book, *Deathbed Visions*, he discovered intriguing aspects that he could not easily explain. For instance, it was fairly common among dying people who had visions to identify friends and relatives that they thought were still alive, but later it was discovered that these people were actually dead. Remember, in those days communication was far slower than it is today. Barrett also found it interesting that children were surprised when they saw angels that they did not have wings. If a deathbed vision was an hallucination you would expect children to see angels in their traditional form.

Further scientific study into such visions was carried out in the 1970s by Dr Karlis Osis for a book entitled *At the Hour of*

Death, which considered thousands of studies and interviews of over a thousand doctors, nurses and relatives who attended the dying. Once again the research uncovered a number of striking consistencies including:

Whether or not a person believes in an afterlife is immaterial.

Most people report seeing loved ones who have passed over.

These loved ones in spirit often tell them that they are there to help them cross over.

The dying person is typically reassured and comforted by these visions.

The dying person's health is sometimes restored temporarily or pain relieved momentarily by these visions.

The experiencer tends to be aware of their real surroundings and does not seem to be hallucinating.

Scientists are keen to argue that deathbed visions are creations of the dying brain – a kind of sedative to ease the dying process – but this does not explain away rare cases, like this one below sent to me by Loraine, when another person also believes they have witnessed something supernatural.

Something mysterious

I'm a hospice worker and I've watched over the deaths of countless men, women and children. Something happened five years ago, though, which completely changed my attitude to the dying process.

I was looking after a man who was brought in one evening. I asked him if he would like me to contact any relatives. He told me that there was only one person he wanted to see, but I couldn't get him to tell me any of her contact details. He told me he had not seen this woman for a long time and I got the feeling that he was talking about a girlfriend or wife who had died many years ago. I couldn't get him to stop talking about her, though, and it took a while for him to fall asleep.

At about ten pm I heard him talking in his sleep in a very loud voice. He was talking about this mystery woman again. I called for more medical help but by the time they arrived he had slipped into unconsciousness. He was unconscious for several hours and I tried to make him as comfortable as possible. I really wished that there was someone I could contact for him but it seemed there was no one. Then at about three in the morning he woke up and became very lucid and alert. This isn't uncommon. I have seen it happen many times when the end is close. He looked at me and then to the other side of the room. I swear I saw the figure of a woman bathed in light standing there. I saw the man's face light up like a torch. He was so very happy to see this woman and it was so moving to see his happiness that I started to cry.

Moments later I saw his arms raised as though someone else had lifted them for him. He took one last breath and as he let it out, his outstretched arms came down and folded across his chest. He died with a broad smile on his face. I would not have believed this had I not seen it with my own eyes. I don't think it was a trick of the light

– I know I saw someone or something standing there waiting for him, and I believe it was the woman he had been talking about. She came to help him cross over. From that day on I have never looked at dying people in the same way. They can see, hear and feel things we can't.

Like many other wonderful souls who care for the terminally ill, Loraine witnesses daily the precious, sacred moment when a person leaves their body behind and she knows that it is a moment of sublime peace and happiness.

All the evidence suggests to me that deathbed visions are exactly what they seem to be: a chorus of angels who come to the dying to ease the transition from this life to the next. And most comforting of all, and proof for many that the hand of heaven is being extended, these striking visions are incredibly reassuring to the relatives and can completely remove the person's fear of dying.

For a dying person deathbed visions can be a source of courage and strength so real that it can even be the catalyst for physical changes. This may be something as simple as a smile, or there may be a burst of energy or the temporary return of sight, hearing or speech. For me, moments of lucidity like this can offer a glimpse of the soul's eternity and the splendour that is still there in the most aged, tired and diseased of bodies.

For William Blake, a poet possessed by angels all his life, death was as simple as 'moving from one room to another'. According to his wife, Blake never lost his faith in the afterlife and spent his dying hours exhausted but happy. The philosopher Søren Kierkegaard also died with a blissful conviction that he was not ending his life but beginning a wonderful journey. According to his nephew:

Never have I seen a spirit break through the earthly husk and impart to it such a glory . . . He took my hand in both of his – how small they were and thin and pale and transparent – and said, 'Thank you for coming and now farewell.' But these simple words were accompanied by a look the match of which I have never seen. It shone out from a sublime and blessed splendour that seemed to me to make the whole room light. Everything was concentrated in those eyes as the source of light and heartfelt love, the blissful dissolution of sadness, a penetrating clearness of mind, and a jesting smile.

Pam also found being present at the death of her mother a more positive experience than she had expected.

A beautiful death

My mum passed away at the age of ninety-seven in October 2010.

I never had a particularly close relationship with my mum – there's no recollection of hugs or cuddles as a youngster. Even though she could be quite severe and stern at times, I do know that she loved me in her way and was always there for me.

Mum was in a nursing home and was extremely frail as well as suffering from dementia. She had not been able to make sense of the world for some time. She was taken to hospital following a medical emergency. Once the medication was sorted and she was pain-free, she slept a lot. I sat for many hours talking to her, uncertain whether, even if she could hear me, she could make any sense of what I was saying. I told her to look forward to the journey she was going on and that it would be a calm and peaceful transition to another magical world. I said there was nothing to be frightened of and that she could do this.

Eventually, when I sensed that perhaps it was near the end, I said, 'If you see Dad say hello for me.' Well, to my amazement she smiled – a huge smile, albeit gummy and toothless! Unbelievably, I hadn't seen a smile for months. I turned to my husband and exclaimed, 'Did you see that?' Then, just to confirm it wasn't a fluke, I said, 'You're going to see Harry soon. He's waiting for you and you're going to see your mum and friends. There's going to be a big celebration and you're going to be the centre of attention. You will have a wonderful time.' Again she gave us this huge radiant smile full of hope and joy. This from someone who barely recognised me and no longer knew that she had been married, let alone that Harry had been her husband. Shortly afterwards she passed away peacefully. She looked calm, pain-free, younger and at peace.

This was the first time I had been present when somebody died and I was totally blown away by how unexpectedly positive the experience had been. I had expected to feel the whole spectrum of grief, but this did not happen and instead I was calm and, to be totally honest, happy. These positive feelings continued to stay with me. When I spoke to my brother in America I told him it had been a privilege to be there with Mum as she passed. I think my friends were concerned that I was not grieving in the traditional way and I did begin to experience a little guilt that my positivity could be interpreted as unfeeling and almost detached.

126

This is where reading your book has really helped me to gain an understanding of what I experienced.

I believe now that we were in the presence of an angel and that's why there were such feelings of joy at what should have been a traumatic time. When I used the word 'privilege' to describe how I felt I shocked myself with my choice of word. I wasn't sure people understood but I couldn't explain it differently. Now I know that the privilege was being with my mum at her special time of passing and in the presence of an angel. This has allowed me to remove any anxieties and to once again celebrate the whole experience, for it was a beautiful death.

Liz sent me this story about the death of her sister, describing how she witnessed a similar joy.

Going home

I was with my sister when she died and I felt closer to her then than I had done for years. She suffered from dementia, you see, and over time it became increasingly difficult to communicate with her. She didn't know who I was any more and suffered violent temper tantrums. It was heart-breaking. In some ways I felt I had lost her years ago, but for a few minutes before she died she came back to me. She sat up and looked at me and said my name. Then she told me I was a wonderful sister but it was time for her to go home now because they were here.

Then she looked to the side and smiled and held out her hand as if someone was going to shake it. She kept looking to her side and holding out her hand for a good minute or so, and then I saw her head lean back against the pillow and her arm gently float down onto the bed beside her, as if someone was placing it there. It was so graceful and so elegant. I knew she had died. She had gone home.

Of course, it is not a given that we all experience such clarity when our moment comes, but even if we don't have such breadth of vision we have no need to spend our final hours riddled with fear. As long as we have faith we can overcome any anxiety.

If you have ever witnessed the final moments of a dying person you may have already sensed the closeness of another realm or presence in the room – call it angels or heaven or eternity. As mentioned earlier in Loraine's story, hospice workers often speak of this experience. Many years ago when I worked part-time in an old people's home I would also witness moments of lucidity and vivid awareness when death approached. I would see faces ravaged by time and pain look young and carefree again. I would see love and I would see happiness and peace. It was indeed a precious, sacred moment.

In this life all we can do is 'see through a glass darkly', but reading about the experiences of others close to death can save our lives in countless ways by reminding us that love is stronger than death, and life more powerful than fear. We discover once again that heaven is not some faraway place, but a reality, even if that reality is an elusive one. I hope what you have read here will have shown you clearly that when a person dies, they awaken to heaven.

Yet unless you are staring death in the face it can be incredibly hard not to see it as a negative thing; our natural instinct is not to think about death as something that will happen to us and those we love. But every morning when we wake up we have no idea whether we have years, days or hours left to live. In the midst of life we are in death, whether we like it or not, and we may never know when our time is up. In other words, you don't know what your final thoughts, words and actions will be, so make sure that your life is filled with love. Let love be the last word in your life.

I truly believe that unless we live for love we will not be able to die with confidence, grace, joy and peace. When our spirits cross over to the other side, I don't think we will be judged on what we have achieved but on how much we have loved. If we fill our hearts with love in this way, we will have truly overcome death.

Grief as an awakening experience

If you've ever lost a loved one you will know what a bitter and shattering life experience it can be, but just as the closeness of death can awaken people spiritually, so too can the experience of grief and loss. Monica's story illustrates this point well, I feel:

Opening up

My sister Melanie died last year and it sent me spiralling into depression. She was younger than me by three years and always the prettier, cleverer one. I was in awe of her and a part of me thought that it should have been me who died as I never sparkled as brightly as she did. Even though she was so special she never, ever made me feel inferior and the two of us were exceptionally close. Rarely a day would go by without the two of us meeting up or chatting on the phone. In some ways she was my other half, my better half.

Before, during and after the funeral I tried to be strong for my parents. They needed me to be strong. Trouble was, all the attention was focused on my parents and I didn't really get any help or support. I was only twenty-one at the time and just didn't know how to fill the void my sister had left behind her. Nothing would ever be the same again for me – no more shared birthday celebrations, anniversaries, holidays or telephone calls telling of the birth of a new nephew or niece. The sharing of life's unique and special events would never be the same again. I'd always been protective of my sister and I wished I had reminded her to wear her seatbelt on the day she died. She'd been picked up by a friend to go to a party and all three girls in the back had died. It was so horribly tragic and wrong.

In the months following the funeral my parents began to turn to me more and more for companionship and support. We'd spend hours talking about Melanie, but instead of helping it just made me feel worse. I started to worry about my own death and what it might do to my parents. Then, about ten months after Mel died, I lost my appetite for food and for life. I missed her so much and couldn't cope with my feelings of guilt, anger, loss, hurt and pain. And then when I was at my lowest point I believe I received three signs in one day from beyond the grave.

The first sign came in a dream. I was asleep and heard very loudly and clearly the voice of a woman saying, 'Everything is going to be

OK now.' When I woke up I knew it had been my sister's voice. The second sign happened that same morning. I was getting up and the scent of roses filled the air, just as they had at the funeral. I had no roses in my bedroom or indeed any flowers in the house at the time. And the third and final sign came when I went round to check on my parents at lunchtime. I really didn't feel I could handle it but then I felt a gentle tug on my right shoulder. There was no one around me at the time and I'm convinced it was Mel saying, 'Come on. I'm OK and you will be too.'

Others can say what they will but I know it was Mel reaching out to me, reassuring me and reminding me that she was alive in spirit and I was still on earth for a reason. I can't say I left all of my grief behind, but it was the start of my gradual recovery. My sister's death has reminded me that whenever there is an ending, there is always a beginning and whenever there is death, there is also new life in spirit. Grieving the loss of my sister was terrifying, but it was also the gateway to my spiritual awakening because I know that a part of us lives for ever.

It can be difficult to understand that the loss of a loved one can lead to the awakening of spirit if you allow yourself to fully experience the loss, but this is exactly what can happen. I know because it happened to me.

When my mum died the grief I felt was out of this world, and made worse by the fact that I didn't appear to get any comforting or reassuring signs from her. I couldn't sense her around me at all and I was wracked with feelings of intense anger, guilt, hurt, loneliness, worthlessness and loss as a result.

What I didn't realise at the time and had to learn the hard way was that I needed to experience all these painful emotions. I needed to work through my grief. I had to learn that grieving for the loss of a loved one does not mean you have lost faith in the afterlife. It simply means you are human and missing physical contact with someone you loved. I had to learn that the joy of reunion in spirit could not occur until I had gone through the pain of grief in the same way a mother feels the pain of labour before the joy of giving birth.

Working through grief simply cannot be achieved without pain and hurt and it does take time, and sometimes a long time but, trust me, the pain does fade and all that will be left is an overwhelming feeling that the love you had for your departed loved one has not died. It is still alive and you will know that your departed loved lives on in spirit.

You may also, as Monica did in the story above, come to a place where you can finally begin to reclaim a part of yourself. When you love someone deeply you give away a part of your spirit and your heart to them and this 'giving over' is a beautiful thing as long as you don't take it to extremes. If you give away too much of yourself, this isn't healthy because you are confusing love with need and lack of self-worth. True love, and the most powerful and healing love of all, is the love that can set a spirit free. So, when a loved one dies, amid all that pain there is also an opportunity to reclaim that part of yourself, the love, creativity and passion you gave to them. Again this will take time but you will eventually find that your strength and passion return to you. You will rediscover who you are in spirit and there can be nothing more empowering and comforting than that.

Again, all this may be hard to make sense of if you are raw with grief, but the death of a loved one can lead to a reawakening of your spirit, a new life for you and a new relationship with your loved one in spirit. This certainly was the case for me. There are some people who seem to be born with a deep spiritual awareness, but for me, the emotional crisis triggered by the loss of my mum opened a psychic door and my angels came rushing in. Prior to that, although I longed to see the world with 'angel eyes', I just couldn't and I needed some kind of jolt to open my eyes and help me see the light. For other people it may not be the loss of a loved one that triggers their spiritual awakening, but a personal crisis such as the end of a relationship, a bout of illness, redundancy or a change in circumstances that triggers a re-evaluation. Or it could be something far less traumatic, like an amazing coincidence, an enlightening dream, the selfless act of a friend or a stranger, a sudden and unexpected 'aha' moment in your life when everything falls into place and begins to make sense again, or the recognition of a deeply personal angel calling card, like a feather, a butterfly, a cloud or a song. All these gentle but reassuring signs from the other side can be triggers for the realisation deep inside you that there is more to this life than what you can see with your physical eyes.

Whatever the crisis, trigger or sign is for you, take comfort in the knowledge that when the time is right for you, your guardian angel will speak to you and it will keep talking until you listen. So, if you don't think your guardian angel has spoken to you yet, just wait and see, because it won't be long before they do. Perhaps your spirit has more to learn on earth before heaven reveals itself to you. Don't try to rush or pressure yourself. Just live your life in a way you know your guardian angel would commend. This doesn't mean you have to be perfect – being perfect is impossible as long as you are human – it means being 'perfectly imperfect' and doing the best you can by living your life with love and goodness in your heart.

Never forget, even if you can't always feel or see them, at whatever age or stage of life you are, in both the bad and the good times, your guardian angel is walking beside you, longing for you to awaken to the love and goodness within and all around you that will keep you safe. The angel will wait silently and patiently until you are ready to be swept off your feet.

CHAPTER FIVE

Dreams That Saved My Life

While we are sleeping angels have conversations with our souls.
Author unknown

The future lies in those who believe in the beauty of their dreams.
Eleanor Roosevelt

As we saw in the previous chapter, near-death experiences and the loss of a loved one can be awakening experiences, but this new millennium offers us all an unprecedented opportunity to wake up to the fact that we are spiritual beings. The ever-increasing number of angel encounters experienced by ordinary people all over the world suggests that the way forward is to become aware that there are many more aspects to our lives than those of the material world.

And one aspect of our lives that we all experience is dreaming. Everyone dreams. Whether we remember them or not we each have about 100,000 dreams over the course of our lives. The only reason most of us think we don't dream is that we haven't got into the habit of remembering our dreams. Dreams fade from our memory almost immediately on waking, so if you want to start recalling your dreams you need to keep a pen and paper by your bedside and as soon as you wake up write down whatever you recall.

Indeed, I strongly urge you to keep a journal of your dreams. You may not realise it but significant messages are constantly being given to you in your dreams and all you need to do is become more aware of them. This awareness may lead to the thought, or perhaps even provide the evidence, that your daily life is not the only reality and when you dream you enter another reality that is boundless. It is well known that some of the world's greatest art, music, literature and inventions have been born out of the magic of dreams and, as you'll see later in this chapter when we discuss premonitions, dreams can also save lives.

Elderly people have often said to me that the older they get, the more their lives seem dream-like. It is sometimes said that when we are in the dream state it is a kind of preparation for when we pass over, as we become aware of life in spirit. And yet despite this, for whatever reason, dreams can sometimes seem so very hard to understand or interpret, but that is simply because the language of dreams is different from our own. It is the language of symbols.

The great majority of your dreams should not be interpreted literally. You need to identify the symbols that appear and see what meaning they have to you. There are plenty of books around to help you understand the language of dream symbols

– and I've written one or two myself – but, although these books can help you unravel the mystery, they can never provide a definitive interpretation. This is because what matters most when it comes to dream interpretation is the personal meaning dream images have for you. For example, if you are afraid of dogs the image of a dog in a dream will have a very different interpretation than it will for someone who adores dogs. So it is always best to think about what your dream symbols mean to you before you consult a dream dictionary.

Powerful symbolic messages are being sent to you all the time in your dreams and dreams really can be incredible tools for self-awareness and spiritual awakening as long as you don't interpret them literally. For example, if you dream of a loved one dying this does not necessarily mean they will die. It may mean they are going through a period of change or transformation or your relationship is changing in some way, because death is a symbol of change. I often think of my dreams as a kind of personal therapist – a way to turn the spotlight on feelings, hopes and fears so that challenges in waking life can be resolved or hidden strength or creativity nurtured.

Symbolic dreams make up the great majority of our dreams. Sometimes you may need to do a bit of self-analysis to get to the real meaning, but it is typically well worth the effort. There are, however, a smaller percentage of our dreams that have a very different feel about them. These dreams are so lucid, intense and obvious that interpreting them literally is the only option. They are also very hard to forget and the images may stay in your mind and heart for days, months or even years afterwards. I call such dreams 'night visions or visitations', because I am convinced they are direct messages from the world of spirit.

The stories that follow in this chapter all fall into the category of night visions or visitations. Each person told me that their nocturnal vision was so clear that the images are permanently imprinted on their heart and the significance of the dream was impossible to ignore. And one of the most powerful and unforgettable of night visions is meeting a departed loved one in your dreams.

Tasha believes she met her father in spirit in a night vision. Here's what she told me.

Someone watching over me

When I was fifteen I had an incredible dream. In my dream I was lying in bed and I knew I was being watched. I glanced up towards the window and my heart nearly stopped as at the window there was a slim man whose face looked very familiar. He smiled at me and placed his hand on the windowpane, as though he wanted to come in. I closed my eyes and when I looked again the man was kneeling down beside me. He had his arms crossed on the bed and his head resting on his arms, and he was watching me sleep. When I looked at him he smiled down kindly at me and just watched me. I sat up with a jerk and woke up.

I told my mum what had happened and she said it was just a dream, but to me it felt so real. Then about a month later my mum and I were looking through some old photographs and I came across a photo of a young man in his early twenties. I recognised him straight away as the man who had visited me that night. I asked my mother who the man in the picture was and she said it was my father when he was in his twenties. She was in disbelief when I told her that he was my mysterious dream-time visitor and said that I must have seen the picture before and just remembered it. I knew that I had never seen that picture before; it was my father visiting me to say he was OK and keeping well.

Kay also met a beloved relative in her dreams, and it changed her mind and her life.

The good life

When I was fourteen I found out I was pregnant. My parents fully supported me and my child was born in June. My nan was taken into hospital in the December. Nan and I had never had much of a relationship, she never said she loved me or showed me any affection, until, that is, she went into hospital. The first time I went to see her I was told she couldn't speak so of course I didn't expect her to say a word. But as I was leaving I gave her a kiss and she said, 'I love you.' That was the first and last time she ever said those longed-for words as she died in the January.

Years later I met my husband. He has a job that takes him away from home a lot, which means it's often me and our three children on our own. At times my life feels a bit low and I often wonder where I will end up and if my marriage will be able to survive the constant struggle of being apart from my husband. I often find myself at the cemetery asking my nan these exact questions, hoping she will tell me.

One night I had a dream that is still very clear to me some years later. In this dream I was walking down a local road with my nan. Both of us were silent until I asked her what my life was going to be like. She told me I was going to have a good life. That was it, the end of my dream, but now every time I feel low, or that things are getting too much, I remember my dream and get the energy to carry on because my nan told me my life will be good. It really gives me comfort.

That's another hallmark of night visions – the dreamer will often wake with a feeling of comfort and hope that they did not have before. This is Hillary's story.

A wonderful man

My father died some forty years ago. He was a wonderful man who spent a lot of time with me and my sister and two brothers. It was devastating to us all when we lost him to cancer, aged forty-nine.

Three years ago I was feeling very depressed and found myself walking along the road thinking, 'I can understand why people commit suicide. Dad, please come and get me.' I was immediately horrified at thinking such a thing and that evening rang my sister-in-law, who is also a great friend. She told me to come over and she put a glass of wine in my hand. It was also assumed I would stay to supper and later that evening her husband went to bed early and we were left sitting talking in front of the log fire. She told me she and my brother had open arms and broad shoulders, that they loved me and I was always welcome there.

I left feeling much better. That night I had the most amazing dream. I was standing outside a huge country house with fields spreading for miles in front of me. It was sunny and the fields had lots of beautiful flowers. Suddenly, my father appeared over the top of the hill. He looked fit and healthy and was smiling. I suddenly realised there were lots of other people I didn't know who he began to chat to. Then suddenly he was standing in front of me. 'Where have you been, Daddy?' I asked. 'Do you have another life somewhere?'

'Yes,' he replied.

'Do you have other children?'

'No, you and your brothers and sister are enough for me.'

'Can I come with you to your new life please?' I asked.

He smiled. 'No, love, it's not your time but you will be all right and I am always with you.' He then walked away and disappeared over the hill. I woke up crying but happy. I knew this was not a dream and that my dad had been sent to talk to me. I later remembered that it was 20 November, his birthday.

I have never forgotten that visit and know that along with my guardian angel, my dad will be there waiting for me when it is my time to go.

There are endless tales of happy and inspiring reunions in the dream state, of meeting up with loved ones who have died. This doesn't surprise me at all because when we are asleep our minds are more open and receptive to receiving messages from

141

loved ones in spirit. Dreams are also one of the gentlest and best ways for loved ones to come back and reassure us without causing unnecessary alarm, especially to those of a nervous disposition. After my mum died I longed to see, hear and feel her but the medium she first chose to make contact with me was through my dreams. Looking back, this was the perfect choice for me because I just wasn't ready for anything else. I had too much fear, anxiety and self-doubt, and that would have closed my mind to any other sign from beyond.

Especially during times of grief, loved ones can make appearances in our dreams. As Elaine's story shows, it is as if they want to ease our pain and offer us support, comfort and a glimpse of hope.

Halfway up the stairs

When I was young I was very close to my grandmother or, as I always called her, 'Nana'. I was always at her house and when I was a young girl if I ever huffed and puffed about a decision Mum made I used to storm off and go sit halfway up the stairs. I could sulk there and still see what was going on in the living room. Let's just say I huffed and puffed and sat halfway up the stairs often.

Now, Nana was always a poorly woman and, sadly, when I was nine she died from throat cancer. I was absolutely broken-hearted but then I started to have this recurring dream and it was a source of great comfort. In my dream I was on the stairs huffing and puffing as usual, but instead of ignoring me this time my mum was telling me to come downstairs because someone special wanted to see me. I remember feeling a little scared but then I came towards the doorway of the living room and saw my Nana. She was surrounded by a golden shining light. She held out her hand towards me and told me not to be afraid. Was this my Nana in spirit form telling me she was OK on the other side?

I wrote back to tell Elaine that this most certainly was her beloved Nana in spirit offering her reassurance that she was OK. And the reason I was so sure was that Elaine told me her dreams eased her pain and were a source of great comfort.

Laura also had a parting dream that quite literally eased her pain.

Dying young

I was nineteen at the time and had been very ill for several years and from the age of nine had undergone five surgeries. I was sick all the time and needed round-the-clock care. I knew I was a source of constant worry and grief to my parents and that they were terrified of my dying young. Then the worst thing you could imagine happened. My little brother went and got himself killed. He was only seventeen and was killed in a freak boating accident on a school trip. All that left my parents was me – crippled and needy and sickly me.

The night after my brother died I cried myself to sleep. A part of me hoped that I would never wake up because real life seemed too hard to bear. Then I had a dream about being in a beautiful wood next to a river that was crystal clear. I can't describe how enchanting and lovely that place was. Best of all I was pain-free. I could walk, run and even fly if I wanted to. The next thing I saw was a brilliant white light coming from above. I got nervous and crouched down and covered my head but then as the light came close I saw that it was my little brother. He was surrounded by an awesome bright light. As soon as I knew it was him I lost all my fear and this loving and peaceful feeling shot through my whole body. The light surrounding him touched my body and then started to melt back into the heavens.

I shot up in bed and gasped for air as if I had been underwater. The next morning I felt stronger and better than I had done in years. I saw how much my parents needed me to get better and be there for them and I was determined to help them in any way I could. I loved them so much. At first I thought it was just a dream but now I know it was much more than that as not only did I cope better with the loss of my brother — I didn't sink into a bottomless pit of despair and hopelessness — but my health improved rapidly from that moment onwards. I wasn't out of the woods yet, and still had three more surgeries to live through, but I did get through them, defying all medical expectations.

I'm fifty-five years young this year and I often meet my departed brother in my dreams. We are closer than ever and I can feel him around me all the time in my waking life. In my dreams he is forever young and I am forever nineteen. It's as if in that first dream I died and was reborn into eternal life.

Gemma also feels comforted by dreams of her grandad in spirit. Here's what she told me:

Two dreams

Having had quite a rocky childhood, witnessing my dad's violence towards my mother and my parents' messy divorce, I had been very close to my grandad, who took on the role of father figure. Sadly, my grandad had rheumatoid arthritis which resulted in him taking his own life. My nan found him and that day marked the onset of her dementia.

I have always had several vivid dreams a night, which I have remembered in minute detail, especially the feelings I have encountered in my dreams. Two dreams that have stuck in my mind for a very long time involve my grandad.

In the first dream I had been involved in a car accident on a dual carriageway and was coming out of unconsciousness, being cut out of the car. My grandad and my uncle, who has also passed, were helping me and I felt inexplicably calm, wondering whether I had died and they were looking after me, taking me to heaven, or whether it was a message to let me know that they were watching over me.

In the second dream, which still seems so real, I'm walking down the garden path from my nan's house (my grandad always used to come with me to see me out). My grandad is sitting on the wall, really happy and smiling with his legs swinging, letting me know he is there and he is looking after my nan. In my dream I am not sure whether the rest of my family can see my grandad but I feel very reassured.

From the moment I woke from both dreams I felt warm and safe and relieved.

Dreams of departed loved ones are also more likely to occur during special anniversaries or birthdays or other dates associated with the departed loved one. Again, as Deborah explains below, it is as if loved ones in spirit want to share these significant days with us.

21 May

21 May is a day I used to dread because it was the day my husband died. It was also our wedding anniversary, so I felt double the pain and grief, but on the night of 20 May, a year after my husband's death, I had this amazing dream. I knew I had to write in to tell you about it.

In my dream I met my husband. It felt so real and vivid. We talked about so many things – our children, our life together, our pet dog. He also told me that our daughter was going to have a little boy. She was pregnant at the time and his prediction turned out to be right. She did have a little boy.

When I woke up the next morning I felt full of hope instead of tears. 21 May had arrived and I wasn't feeling as miserable as I thought I would. I knew it was because of my dream. After that dream I went on to have several more similar ones. They all felt so real. My children told me they were just dreams but I know it was more than that.

My husband always used to be a quiet man in life and in my dreams I think we have talked more than we ever did when he was alive. Also he is the last person I would have thought I would have after-death communication with, because when he was alive he told me he didn't believe in an afterlife. Every time I had a dream of him I woke up feeling energised, not groggy and hazy as I normally do. I feel filled with peace and hope. My children can disagree all they like — I know he appears to me in my dreams.

Deborah makes an important point in her story. After a dream about a departed love one you tend to feel energised. When you wake up you will feel happy and optimistic.

I'm often asked if there is any way you can call a spirit to come to you in your dreams. One way might be to focus all your thoughts on your loved one before you go to sleep. Ask him or her to visit you in your dreams. It will really help if you have got into the habit of remembering your dreams, as this will make it easier for a spirit to reach you. Ask your angels to help the chosen spirit come to you. It may take many attempts and there is always the chance that the spirit will not come, not because they don't want to but because you may not be ready or because they simply don't know how. That is why asking your angels to help you and to guide your loved ones in spirit is important.

Remember, if you aren't sure whether you have had a dream or a night vision or visitation from an angel or a departed loved one, the simple criterion for distinguishing between the two is that a night vision will be brilliantly vivid, feel real and be impossible to forget on waking, as was the case for Natalie:

My dream of heaven

I didn't know how to believe in heaven properly – well, maybe I did.

I couldn't tell because I didn't know what feeling you got when you believed in heaven. So my friend told me that she would pray for me. That night I had a dream about my heaven.

I was walking through a big field of very tall grasses; they were all a lovely golden colour. The sky was a bright blue; it was sunny and warm, not hot or cold – it was the perfect temperature. Everything was perfect. There were thousands of fluffy dandelion seeds and they were getting blown along by the soft warm breeze, as if they were dancing. On my way down the path, I picked up two grasses and I started skipping with them. But one of the grasses blew away and then suddenly a gust of warmish wind blew into my face. It picked me up and I felt as if I weighed nothing. I was being carried as carefully as a mother carries her baby. I felt relaxed and peaceful, far away from reality. I saw the two grasses that I had dropped, I reached out to catch them, I got closer and closer . . .

And then I woke up. It was so clear and I remember every tiny detail and what makes it even stranger is that as soon as I woke up, I knew exactly what it was about. I knew I had dreamt about my heaven.

A night vision will seem as real as your waking life. You may find it hard to believe you were actually dreaming, and every detail is remembered even years later. You don't know how or why but for some reason you just know that this was more than a dream, and if a departed loved one appeared their personality will be so instantly recognisable that there will be no doubt in your mind that they did indeed come to visit you.

Psychologists have come up with all kinds of explanations for parting visions like these, but I've researched enough about them now to know that they are very different from other kinds of dreams. As well as being realistic and impossible to forget, another characteristic that sets them apart is that in almost all cases the dreamer feels comforted by them, or is able to make important changes in their life afterwards. For me this uplifting effect is yet more proof that such dreams are real. When a person is in a state of grief following the loss of a loved one they are often in a swirl of pain, confusion, anger, fear and guilt. It is highly unusual for positive emotions to arise from such negative feelings, making it all the more likely that such dreams come from a higher power. So, if you do have a dream of a departed loved one, don't just write it off as the product of a grieving mind reaching for any kind of relief from the pain and shock of loss. It could very well be that you have received a message from beyond the grave.

Katrina is in no doubt that her grandfather sent her a clear sign that he was very much around. Although it was perhaps not strictly speaking a dream, I'm including it here because it happened at night and because it shows yet again that as far as angel signs are concerned the only rule is to expect the unexpected. Here's her experience:

Tugging at my toes

My grandfather died of lung cancer in March 1988. He was sixty-six; I was twenty-one. My mother and I were very close and I had watched with admiration as she nursed my grandfather for the years he was sick.

I travelled home the day before my grandfather's funeral. I was still extremely unsettled. I asked my mother if I could sleep with her that night – something I hadn't done since I was a small child. She said yes and being in my mother's room made me feel somewhat comforted but I was still a bit spooked. My mother, exhausted from the whole ordeal, fell asleep as soon as her head hit the pillow that night. I eventually fell asleep but awoke to 'something' tugging my big toe. I sat upright. It was pitch black. My toe was still being tugged. Somebody had hold of my big toe. I leant forward and tried to touch whoever was at the foot of the bed. I couldn't reach far enough. Then I quickly pulled my foot away and tried to rationalise what was happening.

I reached over to see if my mother was still in the bed and where her legs were. She was fast asleep. She had her back to me and was tucked up in a ball. I lay there staring into pitch blackness, mystified. Eventually, I cuddled into my mother's back and managed to go back to sleep. In the morning I told my mother what had happened. She was astonished and told me my grandfather, a man of few words, used to wake my grandmother in the mornings by tugging her big toes. He also used to wake his children by tugging their toes when they were young. I had never heard this before.

I believe my grandfather was tugging my toes that night. A huge part of me wishes my mother had been the one to have the experience, but I am happy and grateful it happened to me. After talking to Mum that morning I think we both felt comforted and convinced that Grandad was with us as we prepared to attend his funeral. We still talk about that night and are convinced it was him. I didn't feel spooked after my grandfather's funeral. That feeling was replaced by reassurance that my grandfather is still with us . . .

Then there are incredible stories of parting visions in which the dreamer has absolutely no idea that the person in the dream has died. Nina's story speaks for itself.

Hide and seek

I was taking a nap one afternoon and dreamed of my brother. We were children again playing hide and seek in our garden. It was a warm and sunny day and we didn't have a care in the world. I hid first and my brother found me but then it was his turn to hide and I started to get upset in my dream because I couldn't find him. Then I woke up hearing my brother's voice calling me 'Sis' as he always used to. Half dreaming and half awake, I thought I saw him standing in front of me but then I woke up properly and realised it had been a dream.

My brother was in the army and had recently been stationed in Afghanistan. A day later Mum and Dad got the news we had all been dreading. He had been killed by a roadside bomb – on the same day I had had my dream.

In this next story, although Ed suspected that his wife might not survive he couldn't be certain.

Swinging

My wife was in the second tower to be hit by the planes on 11 September 2001. I was away on business and called her constantly on her mobile but got no response. As the news filtered through about the tragedy I got more and more desperate but still hoped she might have made it out alive. I didn't sleep for two days and when I finally did fall asleep I saw my wife sitting in a swing made of light. She was swinging backwards and forwards and laughing and when I woke up I knew she had gone. I was right. My wife did not survive the Twin Towers but to this day I am not sure if that dream I had was a dream or a vision of her. It felt so real.

Again we get those words – the hallmarks of parting dreams – 'it felt so real'. Ed wasn't alone among the relatives of those killed on 9/11 to have experienced a parting vision. Other relatives reported similar experiences in the chaos and confusion of the immediate aftermath – either a dream of a loved one or a strong feeling of their presence, and many talk of the deep sense of peace that settled on them afterwards. Their loved ones had come to say goodbye.

Dreams of departed loved ones appearing to relatives who don't yet know their loved ones have died are closely related to a category of night visions known as precognitive dreams, or dreams which warn of future events. For me, precognitive dreams offer yet more proof of the existence of an afterlife.

Ever had a dream come true?

Over the years I have come to the conclusion that dreams can connect us with the world of spirit. They can do this because when we sleep the boundaries between our conscious and unconscious loosen, enabling angels to transcend the laws of everyday thinking and the gap between this world and the next. I've also come to the conclusion that some dreams may also be able to bridge the gap between space and time, past, present and future. These precognitive dreams differ from the great majority of dreams, which should be interpreted symbolically, in two important ways. First, precognitive dreams tend to have a clear beginning, middle and end, in contrast to other dreams, which tend to be fragments of unconnected images. Second, precognitive dreams, like parting visions, stand out sharply in their clear and accurate representation of waking life. Jessica's dream is a good example:

Sweet dreams

I used to suffer from nightmares when I was a child. I'd wake up in a ball of sweat, shrieking. I'd see monsters and all sorts of scary things. I think a lot of that was due to with the fact that I saw my mum being knocked about by my dad and I was taken into care at the age of six. I was one of the lucky ones, though, because I was adopted by the most amazing parents. I call them parents because that is what they have become to me.

It took a while for me to trust adults but gradually I let down my guard and life got easier. I also had fewer and fewer nightmares. I'm thirty years old now and rarely have them at all. In fact, I don't think I even dream much. I never remember anything when I wake up. There is this one dream I had, though, that I did remember clearly on waking and I want to tell you about it.

I have a four-year-old son and my greatest fear is that I will lose him or that something will happen to him. So when I had this dream that I was in a supermarket with my husband and we lost him you might have expected me to wake up panicking, but quite the opposite – I woke up relieved that the dream wasn't real. I didn't think anything about it until the next day when I was shopping with my husband and I glanced back at him and noticed him bending down to tie his shoelace. Now normally that would have been nothing unusual, and I would not have thought anything about it and carried on shopping, but that was exactly what had happened in my dream. We had both been in a supermarket and my husband had bent down to tie his shoelace but when he got up our son was gone. Heeding the warning my dream had clearly given me, I looked around and noticed that our son was happily skipping around a corner towards the comics and sweets counter. My husband was busy selecting apples from the baskets and hadn't noticed our son skip away.

I dread to think what might have happened if I hadn't had that dream. I thank my angels every day. I don't think of dreams any more in terms of nightmares and panic attacks. I think of them as 'sweet dreams'.

Jessica's dream left her in a state of complete awe at the power of her dreaming mind and the invisible celestial beings that help us in our lives. Such a chillingly accurate dream as the one Jessica had is rare, but a similar case is this dramatic dream reported by the *Washington Daily News* back in 1967. According to this newspaper a mother in Karachi, Pakistan dreamt on 7 May that an elderly man dressed in white told her to dig up the grave of her two-year-old daughter, fifty hours after she had been buried. Her friends told her it was nothing but a dream but this didn't stop the mother going to the cemetery to open the grave. The child was found alive and sucking her thumb when the grave was opened. The mother's precognitive dream had saved her child's life.

Then there are all those people who have written to me to tell me that they had dream premonitions of natural or man-made disasters, such as earthquakes or the attacks on the Twin Towers. Sadly, disaster wasn't averted in these cases, because typically when people had their dreams they had no idea something like this could ever happen, but again such dreams prove that when we dream we really can cross the boundaries of time and space. Santiago sent me this story.

Falling down

On the night before 9/11 I couldn't sleep, which was strange because if you ask my family they'll tell you I always sleep like a log. I just had this feeling of foreboding along with a tightness in my chest. I eventually fell asleep but woke up with this vivid dream in my head.

In my dream I was on top of a large high-rise building in New York. I was looking down on roads and highways, watching people go about their business. Then the building started to collapse underneath me, so without a hint of fear or uncertainty I decided to jump off. When I jumped off the falling building, instead of falling I found myself flying. I awoke full of peace and a vivid memory of this dream, which I wrote down, as I do with all my memorable dreams, to see if they have significance that can be identified in the future. A couple of hours later, I heard about the terrorist attack and turned on the television. I saw the destruction. What I saw corresponded with my dream scene remarkably.

As I said, such dramatic precognitive dreams are very rare. More common are dreams that are not accurate replicas of future events, but representations of *potential* futures. Although they may not be as newsworthy they are no less awe-inspiring as they offer us opportunities to experiment with possible courses of action, or change the course of events to avert problems or disaster. And, as Jane's story below shows, you don't necessarily have to be asleep to experience precognitive visions. They can occur both when our eyes are shut and when they are wide open.

Indelible impression

I am a capable person who is used to driving around at night, on my own, in the very rural area where we live in the south of England. One night, a few months ago, something happened that convinced me of the existence of second sight or my guardian angel or enhanced intuition. Call it what you will, the experience made an indelible impression upon me and, I am convinced, saved me from coming to serious harm.

I had been at a meeting of my book club and left at about eleven pm to begin the fifteen-mile drive home. I was driving down a very narrow lane in an unpopulated area, feeling quite comfortable, when a very strong fear came over me. It wasn't a general reaction to the environment, which, after all, is very familiar to me. This was a very specific fear and it came with a strong pre-knowledge, an image of something that was about to happen. What I saw in my mind's eye was so clear that my flight-or-fight instinct kicked in and I felt my heart begin to pound as I prepared myself to cope with what I felt certain lay a little further along the road.

Turning back wasn't an option; I knew I had to keep going but I also knew that I mustn't stop the car. What I had been given – it felt like information that had been downloaded to my brain as a complete package of insight – was the knowledge that around the corner a man was going to try to stop the car and cause me harm. I also knew he would be coming from the right-hand side, level with my driver's door. I drove on for another mile, all senses alert. As I rounded a corner and approached a bridge I could see him: a man, by the side of the road, by his car, which had been pulled over to the right side of the road, just where I knew he was going to be. As I approached I found myself knowing that I would keep on driving, whatever happened. I also had a second self in the back of my head playing the version of the story that would be happening in which – had I not received the information – I would now be slowing down to see how I could help.

Anyway, as I drove past him the man suddenly leapt forward and bashed his fist onto my driver's window with a really dark and menacing look on his face. Shaken, and with my adrenalin level now soaring, I continued to drive past and looked back to see him standing in the middle of the road staring at my car. Even now, writing this, I can feel my heart tighten at the recollection. I've often experienced insightful moments, and strange coincidences, but this is by far the strongest yet. My father died when I was eleven and cannot shake the thought that he was there that night, keeping me safe.

As I said above the purpose of such precognitive flashes is to reveal potential futures if we follow a certain course of action. In this way they indicate possibilities and show that our future is not fixed. This includes dreams that warn of impending danger because when the dreamer recognises in real life the events already seen in their warning dream they are often able to make changes. Here's Gary's story.

Head on

A few years ago I was a travelling salesman and I was on the road a lot. One night I had this really vivid dream. I was driving down a road I did not recognise. I passed a church and then came to a sharp corner. Before I had a chance to slow down the headlights of an oncoming car appeared in front of me. The car was travelling very fast and I woke up at the moment of impact.

The dream was frightening but after a few days I forgot all about it, until I found myself driving in the south of England down a road

I had never travelled before. But it wasn't really unfamiliar. I had seen it in my dream. Things got really eerie when I saw the church that had appeared in my dream and, sure enough, there was the sharp bend in the road just after the church. It was exactly how I had dreamed it. In an instant I found myself slowing right down and as I did this other car came hurtling around the corner at a crazy speed. Seconds later a police car followed in hot pursuit.

Now, that police car hadn't been in my dream but everything else had: the road, the church, the sharp bend and the speeding car coming around it. I truly believe that my dream allowed me to take evasive action just in time to avoid a head-on collision. It was a miracle.

Gary's story reminds us that we all have the ability to change our future and avert potential danger, conflict or problems by the actions we take in the present, the here and now. Sometimes, though, life doesn't give us any warning and the danger presented to us is very clear and immediate, as this next story from Sam sent to me five years ago illustrates so well.

The rocking chair

I'm fifty-six now and I can still remember this dream I had when I was seven years old with absolute clarity. If I hadn't dreamed it I might not be writing to you today.

At the time, I was sent to stay with my aunt and uncle for the summer holidays, in their isolated cabin-style house in Massachusetts, while my parents went on a second honeymoon. I loved staying with them. It felt like going camping but with all the homely comforts.

An Angel Saved Me

Anyway, back to my dream experience. I woke up one morning feeling really ill. I was down with a cold, but it wasn't just your basic common cold. It felt worse than that, with sneezing, watering eyes, and coughing. My uncle went to work during the day and my aunt stayed at home with me. By the afternoon my cold had escalated to a very bad fever. We ran out of cough syrup, and my aunt had to go get some more. I knew that she was hesitant to leave me all alone, but back in the early 1950s parents and family were more relaxed about leaving children to their own devices, and my cough had become so bad that she had no choice. So she left, saying she would be back within the hour.

Coughing so much quickly exhausted me and I must have fallen asleep. As soon as I drifted off, I had a dream. It was about a little boy. The boy had stringy brown hair and huge blue eyes. I have never seen anyone like him before or since. Anyway, the boy was sitting in a rocking chair. Then, he looked up and I saw his amazing blue eyes again. He said in a loud, rich voice, a voice I wouldn't think belonged to a child at all, 'Time to leave now.' I woke up then. I was sweating and breathing hard and fast. I got up and went downstairs to see if my aunt had come back. I didn't want to be alone.

While I was walking down the stairs I smelled smoke. I ran as fast as I could out of that house. And, when I turned, I saw it go up in flames. Bright red, orange, and yellow touched the skies. I was amazed and frightened all at once. The flames amazed me. The little boy from my dream intrigued me. I knew it was only a dream but he had felt so real.

· As it turns out, there was some soup left on the back burner. The burner was left on, and it had spilled over. I guess something was

160

wrong with the electrical wiring in the stove, and it just blew up after the pot had bubbled over in the circuits.

As I said, to this day half a century later, I'm convinced that that dream saved my life. That little boy's face is quite literally forever burned into my memory.

It could be said that stories like this are simply about intuition or survival instinct, but it could also be said that intuition is a form of premonition in that it is an early warning sign of future events. And premonitions that save lives or avert disaster, whether they occur in dream form or manifest through the voice of our intuition, are, I believe, heaven-sent. They are also far more common than many of us think. People have had premonitions throughout recorded history. For example, many of the passengers on the ill-fated *Titanic,* which struck an iceberg and sank in 1912, reported having premonitions about the ship. Some of them heeded these warnings, but others didn't. One of the reasons many of us ignore these warnings is that they are typically too subtle to register in our conscious minds. They are not noticed or recognised as premonitions until after the event comes to pass, when the realisation hits like a ton of bricks. Again that is why premonitions tend to occur more often when we are in the dream state and our unconscious mind reigns supreme.

People who have visions of the future, otherwise known as precognition, are often said to be psychic or to have supernatural abilities, meaning they are able to experience something that does not conform to the laws of physics, or so-called normality.

But, in my opinion, the only reason that something is described as psychic or supernatural is our lack of understanding. But that is another book. What I am trying to say is that you don't have to be psychic to have a premonition, just as you don't need to have supernatural abilities to see, hear and feel angels. All you need to do is pay more attention to your gut feelings or intuition and, of course, your dreams.

This next story from Eve is thought-provoking.

The school trip

For days before the school trip to a zoo my six-year-old daughter, Saffron, was over the moon with excitement. She wanted to be a vet when she grew up and couldn't wait to spend a day with her friends and the animals. We'd taken her to a zoo before, but she had only been two or three at the time and perhaps not quite ready for it.

The night before the trip Saffron went to bed early so that the next day would come sooner. I remember tucking her in and she was so excited. The next morning, though, brought something unexpected. Saffron didn't want to go. She told me she wasn't feeling very well. She said she had a tummy ache, but she didn't have a temperature and wasn't coughing or sniffing so it didn't make any sense. I tried to get her out of it by bringing her breakfast in bed and letting her watch TV but she still did not want to go. Short of dragging her out of bed I was forced to ring the school and say she wouldn't be coming in.

During the day Saffron was much quieter than usual. She slept in the morning and then in the afternoon she got some of her energy back. I gave her some colouring pens and paper while I was doing the ironing and before I knew it she was drawing frantically. I didn't pay much attention until it was time to clear up. I saw that all her pictures were of cars and buses crashing into each other. I asked her what this was all about and she said she had had a dream of her school coach crashing. Suddenly, everything made sense and I spent the rest of the afternoon telling her that it was only a dream and nothing bad was going to happen.

Later that evening I received a phone call from the mum of one of Saffron's friends. She was fairly shaken and told me that the school bus had been involved in an accident on the way home from the zoo. Mercifully, no one was seriously hurt and apart from a few cuts and bruises they were all OK. My Saffron was the only child that day not on the school trip and I wanted to ask if you think she knew something might happen. Did she have a dream about the accident before it happened? This kind of thing has never happened to us before and I'm keen to know more so I can help Saffron deal with what I think may be her 'gift'.

Writing back to Eve, I told her that it is certainly possible her daughter's dream was the warning kind, or a glimpse of future events. I told her that her daughter's gift could become a guiding force for the rest of her life. You might be wondering what the big deal was, because the school bus accident was not serious, but when you think about the idea that we are all connected and nothing we do or say is trivial, it is possible that if Saffron had got on the bus this may have changed the timing of the accident in some way that could have caused tragedy.

In other words, there may have been an important reason for her forewarning.

Bridget is convinced there was an important reason for her premonition — it saved her life and that of her little brother.

The wall

I was walking home from school with my little brother, who was holding my hand. It was a few weeks before Christmas. The roads were quite slippery and it was very busy. I remember walking beside a wall with a nice bricked top that my brother loved to climb up on and walk along. There were two women in front of us and the street was fairly narrow and I remember feeling a bit frustrated because we weren't walking fast enough and it was hard for my brother to keep his balance at such a slow speed. Suddenly, a feeling of dread came over me. It felt as if someone was pouring ice-cold water down my back. I stopped in my tracks with my brother wobbling on the wall. He asked me what the matter was and a couple of people barged angrily past me but nothing was going to make me move. I couldn't. I really couldn't. I was frozen. This went on for a good thirty seconds. Then I heard a roaring sound. I knew what was going to happen. A bus was going to crash into the wall.

I jumped out of my trance, grabbed my brother around the waist and moved as far back on the street as I could. At that moment a bus came crashing into the wall at the exact spot my brother and I had been standing. There were several people trapped there and seriously injured and I later found out that one of them died. It makes me shudder to think it could have happened to us too.

In some inexplicable way Bridget was touched by an invisible dimension and, lost there for a moment in time, she was given the insight and the foresight to save herself and her little brother from serious injury – even death. She has no idea why she was saved that day and why others had to die. Did they perhaps receive a warning they ignored? Or were there higher reasons for the fates of all those involved? For Bridget the miracle is that it was not her time to die that day.

Among the most intriguing precognitive dreams are those about meeting children before they are born. These dreams, which often include detailed and accurate information about a child's future personality or appearance, sometimes even before conception, are just incredible but I have no reason to doubt that, like all the other incredible stories in this book, they are heaven-sent. Here's what Nadine told me:

A story about Hope

I lost my beloved mother to cancer in December 1989 and before she died I promised her that if I should have a daughter I would call her Hope and she would be our hope for the future. In the middle of 1992 I found out I was pregnant, which was a surprise, as I was just recovering from my second ectopic pregnancy and I had been told I wouldn't be able to have any further children due to all the scarring. I was really fretting, even after the doctors had confirmed that the baby was in the right place and was doing fine. I couldn't get rid of the fear of something going wrong with this baby.

Then when I reached about seven months I started to have these dreams in which I could hear a baby crying and I could see the baby, but I wasn't allowed near it. I would wake up crying and frustrated as I wasn't allowed to settle this baby. I had this dream every night for over a month. Two weeks later I asked my mum in spirit to somehow let me know what was going on as it was breaking my heart. That night I had the dream again but this time I was allowed to go to the cot and look at the baby and I saw this little dark-haired baby girl and my mother was standing next to the cot smiling.

After I woke up I felt at peace and I didn't have the dream again. But on 8 May 1993 I went into labour and after eight hours it was time. Well, you know how things go, my baby arrived but hadn't cried and my husband said, 'Hope is here. Hope has arrived.' I didn't believe him, but the nurses confirmed what he had said. Then my baby cried, and it was the same cry from my dreams. When they laid her in my arms I knew it was the same baby and I felt a hand take the weight off my shoulders. A week later when I returned home from hospital, sitting on my dressing table in my bedroom was an old photograph. It was a baby photograph of my mother and I noticed how my daughter and my mother look exactly the same.

Aron also had a vision of his child before he was born. His astonishing story of survival against all odds, and the vision which saved him, have recently been recorded in a riveting bestselling book, *Between a Rock and a Hard Place,* now made into the Oscar-nominated film *127 Hours* directed by Danny Boyle, and if you haven't read the book or seen the film here's a brief taster:

Salvation

Trapped for an excruciating 127 hours between a boulder and a rock wall, experienced mountaineer Aron Ralston amputated his own arm to save his life. After his ordeal Aron made constant references to experiencing 'an epiphany' and 'a miracle'. He said salvation came when he had a vision of a small boy who gave him the will to live. In his book he describes the boy in detail as his future son. He hadn't then met his wife but months later he did and she later gave birth to a boy, Leo, who fits the description exactly. Ralston is quoted as saying, 'Love: at the deepest point that's what connects us', and he has gone on to make a mockery of his disability. Since the accident he has scaled all fifty-nine peaks over 14,000 ft in Colorado and climbed Kilimanjaro. He took the decision to make the accident the turning point of his life, which is why he decided to write a book about it so his story could touch other people. It was a gift to his son Danny. Today Aron lives in Colorado . . . in a town named Boulder.

Stories like Aron's are truly awe-inspiring, and whenever I read it I am reminded of the evidence it offers that we are all spiritual beings with the ability to cross the boundaries of space and time, life and death. Even if it is only in our dreams, or for one brief moment in our waking lives, we can all touch upon something we know to be greater and more important than ourselves. A medical person might use complicated terminology to explain such experiences, but none of these terms or explanations can ever capture the 'truth' of the moment for the person concerned.

Perhaps the genius of artists, musicians and writers, or the joy experienced by lovers or first-time parents, or the explorer soaring to new heights, comes close to the inspiration of feeling 'not of this world'. But what of those whose hearts are broken, or who are on the edge of despair, and have suddenly and surprisingly found themselves led to the light and discovered a new sense of hope and peace? They just know, without a shadow of a doubt, that their experience was real, proving that otherworldly light can shine down on us both in moments of elation and in moments of darkness. Our angels can reach out to us in both our joy and our anguish.

Out-of-body experiences

There is another type of night-time adventure that has me convinced that there is more to us than our physical bodies, and that is the out-of-body experience, or OBE.

Some people seem to be able to induce an out-of-body experience through techniques such as meditation or visualisation, but from my research I have found that OBEs are more likely to happen involuntarily and much to the surprise of the person involved. Many people say they have had the sensation of floating or flying near the ceiling or seeing their physical body beneath them. In common with night visions, people say that the experience feels very vivid and as if it is happening in the real world. The event is remembered clearly for many years afterwards.

There is some crossover between OBEs and near-death experiences, in that near-death experiencers often report the sensation of leaving their body, but out-of-body experiencers do not include the fact (or the belief) of being close to death. In short, with an OBE the physical body is typically not in danger or trauma and OBEs tend to happen at the most unexpected times, and in the most spontaneous ways. I can testify to this.

I've only had two out-of-body experiences. The first happened when I had just had my second child at the age of thirty-five – like all my psychic experiences it came to me fairly late in life. I don't know how or why it happened but I remember looking down on myself as I slept at night. I noticed that my nightdress was on back to front and when I found myself back in my body I discovered that was indeed the case. The second happened three years ago when I was giving a short talk about angels at my local bookshop. I don't often give talks, because I believe people will be guided to my books rather than led to them by publicity, but generally when I do decide to give a talk it turns out to be a pleasant experience and the people who meet and greet me are warm and welcoming. This time, though, I wasn't enjoying the experience at all and the atmosphere didn't feel right. I wasn't getting through to my audience and the words were not flowing. Indeed, a part of me wished I wasn't there.

Then something extraordinary happened. I was halfway through attempting to answer a tough question when I suddenly saw myself from the audience's point of view. It was as if I was sitting in a seat in front of me. There was no sensation of leaving my body, just that I was suddenly watching myself. I was conscious that I watched myself for a few seconds before the sensation melted away and I was back in my body. When I was out of my body I remember wondering what I might say next to the audience. Would I be able to keep talking and interacting while I was watching myself? I was conscious that I was thinking of myself in the third person, as if I was commenting on someone else.

The other incredible thing is that when I found myself back in my body all my feelings of discomfort had gone and the words flowed so much that the bookshop owner had to politely tell me it was time to wind things up. People often come up to me to ask questions or say things after a talk, but in this case virtually everyone who attended wanted to speak to me. They all said that my books meant something specific to them and told me their stories of angelic encounters or talked about their belief in angels. It was remarkable.

Quite a few people have written to me to tell me about OBEs occurring when they were speaking or performing on stage, and it seems this may have been the case for me three years ago in that bookshop. Musicians seem to be especially prone to the experience. Others report having OBEs while jogging or praying or reading or daydreaming, but by far the most common time is during sleep or when a person is lying down preparing to go to sleep and they enter that twilight world between consciousness and unconsciousness.

Daryl's experience happened when she was a teenager.

Unravelling

I was lying on my bed daydreaming about something or other and felt very sleepy. The next thing I knew I had this sensation of accelerating at great speed as if I was on a roller-coaster. I willed myself to stop and found that I was floating above my body. I was looking down at myself. It didn't feel weird or surprising but perfectly normal, as if this was the way things were meant to be. My thoughts were under my control but my body wasn't. I could not move it. I could see that I was lying on my back and that my ponytail had unravelled. Then I saw my sister walk into my room, go to the wardrobe and grab one of my tops. Then she left the room, quietly closing the door. I had this rushing, speeding sensation again and I felt myself floating higher, but I got scared and the moment I got scared I was back in my body waking up.

I got up and noticed that my hair was a mess. Then I checked in my wardrobe and sure enough my top was missing. I have never had an experience like this before or after. I'm thirty-three now and fascinated by all things spiritual and would love to have the experience again. I've made a promise to myself that if it does happen again I won't let fear stop me flying higher.

Phil describes his OBE as truly mind–shattering.

Out cold

This happened during a routine operation in hospital. I was given a general anaesthetic so I know I was out cold, but I realised I was out of my body watching the operation. I was hovering close to the ceiling. The moment I realised what was happening I was jerked back into my body and waking up from the operation. I could, however, describe every detail of what occurred during the operation – who came in and out of theatre, what was said and so on. I think the accurate details I gave him convinced my doctor that what happened to me was real. Many people have asked me what the experience felt like and it is hard to describe. The best I can say is that it was truly mind-shattering and no experience on earth can match it. I didn't feel anything. It was just me. I was pure, liberated and free. I was authentic. I felt real at last.

Ken's experience has convinced him that love can never die, even when our bodies do.

Stepping out

My mother died in 2008; we were very close and I grieved perhaps more than most. A few weeks after her death, though, we met in my dreams. I went to sleep and suddenly found myself stepping outside my body. It felt perfectly natural to do this, as if I was simply taking off a heavy coat. Then I floated to the ceiling of my bedroom, drifted through the roof and at great speed travelled across lands and seas and ended up on a beach in Hawaii. My mother was waiting for me there. She took my hand and told me she was happy where she was and that this would be the last time I saw her. Then she smiled at me and walked away and as she did she began to fade, first her arms and legs, then her body, then her head and the last to fade away was her eyes. I stood for a while watching the waves lap on the shore. The next thing I knew I was waking up in my bed.

The dream helped me through my grief in so many ways. I knew it was my mum's way of saying goodbye. She had always longed to visit

Hawaii but never had when she was alive. Now in spirit she was there. She was happy. She was OK.

Scientists like to explain that OBEs are caused either by chemical changes in the brain, or by the desire of the individual to compensate for the loss of a loved one by creating dream images of them, but, again, I don't find their arguments in any way conclusive. I am convinced that Ken did indeed have an OBE because the difference between a symbolic dream and an out-of-body dream is considerable, with the clarity, above all, of Ken's experience making it the latter kind. Undoubtedly, Ken had an OBE, in which state he was as much part of the spirit world as his mother.

No matter how hard researchers and psychologists study the human mind to explain things like consciousness, dreams, memory, feelings and OBEs, explanations will not be found because the brain is not the source of these things, just as a TV is not the source of the images produced. There is no proof that OBEs, or any supernatural experience for that matter, originate in the brain. In my opinion, OBEs, just like night visions and NDEs, offer credible testimony that we are indeed spiritual beings inhabiting physical bodies.

There are many different names given to the spiritual part of us that can travel outside our body and these include astral body, dream body and, my favourite, soul body. OBEs themselves have also been called astral projection, dream travel and even boarding the spiritual plain. Many people argue that OBEs are simply dreams but, as we saw earlier, dreams are profound messages from the other side, and to anyone who has had an OBE – and from the research I have done and the number of stories I receive I know there are thousands of you – the experience can be even be more powerful than a dream and become a deep and rich source of spiritual awakening.

Sleep worker

And now that we have returned to the subject of spiritual awakening, I want to finish this chapter with a brief mention of another exciting category of night-time dreams. These are what I like to call spirit worker, or spiritual assignment, dreams, and they are closely linked to out-of-body experiences in that the people who have them say that when they fall asleep their spirit bodies leave their physical bodies to undertake spiritual tasks or assignments. These assignments can vary widely, but typically involve helping people pass over to the other side, or offering people hope and strength during times of crisis.

When I first heard about these kinds of dreams several decades ago I thought they were nothing more than remarkable dreams, but over the years I have been sent numerous stories, like this one below from Daisy, which have convinced me they are valid and real experiences.

Crying out

Last year I had a dream about a woman I have never met. In my dream this woman was giving birth. I was present in the delivery room with her and her husband and I witnessed their intense grief when their stillborn child was handed to them. I found myself reaching out to comfort them. I placed my hands on their shoulders and then I saw that their baby was crying. They didn't seem to notice. I tried to tell them that their baby was alive but they could not hear me. The baby kept on crying and it broke my heart so I reached out and placed a hand on the baby's forehead. Immediately the crying stopped and the baby looked at me and smiled. After a while the parents placed the baby in a small cot beside them and hugged each other. I went over to the baby and picked him up. He was a beautiful baby boy and I danced around the delivery room with him. Then I saw a bright light open up in front of me and two figures stepped out from it and held out their hands. I knew I had to give the baby to them. The baby was sleeping peacefully so I kissed him on his forehead and handed him over. Then I woke up.

My dream has helped me in so many ways, especially last October when my sister had a stillborn baby girl. I was with her in body rather than in spirit during the delivery, but I know that there was someone there for my little niece when she crossed over.

Daisy has no idea why she was present at the passing over of someone she did not know, but I suspect it may have something to do with the fact that in spirit we are all family. The important thing is that her experience was a source of incredible comfort to her because it convinced her when her sister's baby died that the little girl was not alone either.

If dreams are a way for our consciousnesses to learn, grow and develop in our sleep it is highly likely that those of us who are drawn to the idea of angels, or to helping others in our waking lives, will also be drawn to spiritual or healing work in our dreams. But it isn't just people who are spiritually inclined who have these kinds of dreams – anyone can have them. I have received accounts of such dreams from people in a variety of different professions, from doctors to teachers, accountants, solicitors, nurses, social workers, stockbrokers and, yes, even traffic wardens and investment bankers. Some say that several times a year they have dreams in which they find themselves at the service of those in need.

I don't have any memory of spiritual assignment dreams myself, but I do have lots of experience of waking up feeling worse for wear for no good reason after a good eight or so hours' sleep. Perhaps this has happened to you also on occasion? There may be medical or emotional or physiological reasons – which should, of course, be checked by a doctor – but if you can't think of any good reason why you feel tired you may want to consider the possibility that you have been doing a great deal while you were sleeping. Perhaps you were there helping someone cross over to the other side, offering comfort and companionship when they needed it the most, or perhaps you were empowering others or offering them courage, hope and comfort in some invisible way. It is the most wonderful thought that when we sleep we may all have the potential to grow wings and become angels walking alongside those in need.

While you were sleeping

It is such a shame then that so many of us barely pay any attention to our dreams. We are so preoccupied with the business and excitement of our daily lives, but I hope this chapter will have shown you that our night-time adventures can be even more exciting, because when we fall asleep and dream, the barriers of logic, time, place, disbelief and negativity are lifted, giving our spirits a chance to soar. We have far greater access to our vast spiritual potential when we are dreaming than when we are awake, so I urge you all to pay more attention to your night-time journeys.

Should any images that appear in your dreams feel upsetting or frightening, don't let them disorientate you because in almost every case nightmares are not meant to be interpreted literally, but symbolically. Your dreaming mind is using powerful and dramatic imagery to alert you to certain aspects of your daily life which might need rethinking, or drawing your attention to potential areas of conflict within or around you. Your dreaming mind wants you to take positive action and may have to resort to scare tactics if you have ignored more subtle warning signs from your angels in the past. Remember, the purpose of dreams is to help set you on the right path.

And if you have a night vision, or an OBE, remember that it will always feel very different from normal dreams that need to be interpreted symbolically. You will feel energised, reassured and comforted. There will be no fear or uncertainty, just

a quiet knowing of the truth – a truth that can help your spirit
soar.

I could linger much longer on angel communications through
dreams but there isn't time and space here . . . perhaps next time.
Until then I think this sweet poem sums things up:

<u>*Sweet dreams*</u>
A loving angel came to me in dreams,
And showed me life's not always what it seems,
And brought me to a place where sweet dreams live,
And gave to me a gift that I now give:

She whispered, 'Take my hand, I'll lead you through
A place where all the sweet dreams can come true!
Close your eyes and open up your heart,
For then this flight of dreams so sweet can start.'

She brought me through the darkness to the light,
Where colours wrapped around me with delight,
A patchwork quilt of beauty without seams,
Each colour was a rainbow full of dreams.

She led me through a hall of lovely sound,
With doors flung open widely all around.
And from each room a song would gently play,
And I wished with all my heart that I could stay.

Dreams That Saved My Life

We drifted in the fragrance of the breeze,
To savour all the flowers and the trees.
We tasted all of life that we could see,
And felt it flow as one in harmony.

Then my angel turned to me and said,
'You're the keeper of these dreams inside your head.
Dream sweetly now, and dream of love and light,
And dreams will lead you safely through the night.'

I am the keeper of this dream, it's true,
And I offer all my dreams to each of you.
May their loving sweetness visit you each night
And fill your soul with love and warmth and light!

Author unknown

CHAPTER SIX

Moments of Enchantment

There is a desire deep within the soul which drives man from the seen to the unseen, to philosophy and to the divine.

Kahlil Gibran

If it happens, it is possible.

An unnamed law of the universe

<u>Open Your Mind</u>
I live deep within your mortal soul
I see all your life as it unfolds
I'm the angel you may not see
But I will always hold you close to me

Through the good times and the bad
I will give you strength you thought you never had
So open up your mind to me
I'm here for all eternity

Jim O'Donnell

Moving from dreams to delve more deeply into the meaning of real-life experiences, we could perhaps begin by questioning 'reality' itself.

What exactly is reality? Is it a given moment in time – the moment we are experiencing right now, not yesterday or tomorrow, but right now? But what if we are remembering yesterday or dreaming about tomorrow in the present moment? Is reality all life's experiences from the moment we are born? If it is, does that reality include dreams, near-death experiences, out-of-body experiences and other angelic encounters? Is reality the moments in time when we are awake? If it is, what happens when we go to sleep and move into the world of dreams? Are we not real then and simply transitioning to another state of being?

Or is the very moment of experience – whatever that experience may be – our reality? If it is, and I believe it is, then whenever we see, hear or feel angels, that moment of enchantment is as real as any other moment in our life. It is another reality.

All the people who submitted the stories for this chapter believe that they caught a glimpse of this other reality and that glimpse, however brief, was enough to save or transform their lives with an inner knowing that helped them move mountains. A sense that reassured them that no matter how hard their lives got, or how disillusioned, forgotten or sad they felt, there is always a higher power there for them.

And just as those who have had near-death experiences are transformed, becoming more courageous and spiritual as a result, so too many people who have experienced moments of enchantment say that they have discovered strength and power within themselves. They talk of feeling 'warm and comforted' or 'reassured that they are not alone' or 'convinced that all will be well'. Often, though, they find themselves at a loss for words to describe their moment of transformation, the moment in their lives when they discover that there is no other reality than their belief and trust in angels.

In my work I am constantly overwhelmed and delighted by the sheer number of people who interact with angels on a daily basis. Many of these people, like Jeanette whose story is below, believe they can sense angels all around them.

The sanctuary

I have seen an angel standing at the bottom of my bed. It was around the date Mum would have been gone for a year. This angel just stood there. She was barely visible, apart from her outline. My room felt full of the presence of beauty. The angel came to tell me that Mum and Shaun (a family friend who passed a week after Mum) were OK. She didn't simply vanish, she glided away, and as she glided she got fainter and fainter.

My bedroom is the place where my husband passed over. I still have our bed and I call this room my sanctuary because that is exactly what it feels like. When you walk into this room you just feel peace. I know this is the place where those who love me in spirit are, and where my angels come to visit me.

As you'll see in her story below, Cheryl also walks with angels, even though her life has felt incredibly difficult at times.

Walking with angels

I got married in June 1988, and the marriage was going well. In 1992 our first child, a girl, was born and I felt my family was complete, but in 1994 we decided to try for another baby as I hated the idea of my daughter being an only child. Thankfully heaven graced me with another pregnancy and we were both thrilled.

Five months into the pregnancy there were complications. I was told that my baby was not developing properly and that the chances of the baby surviving were very slim. On 2 June 1994 my son Stephen was born, but sadly he was called back to heaven within an hour of his birth. We were devastated. I am sure you have heard the saying that when God takes a life he also gives a life, and to our surprise and joy in July 1995 our second daughter was born.

At this stage I was delighted with my family but still very upset over my son and my grief was putting a strain on our marriage. In 1998 my husband wanted to leave Dublin and move down the country. I was happy where I was but in May of 1999 we moved to a little village in Wexford where my husband bought the local shop. It was then that someone introduced me to angel cards. I was fascinated by them and thought that they were fantastic. The following year a lady came into the shop. She had just lost her husband and I decided to give her my set of angel cards, the first that I had ever bought – there was a part of me that did not want to give the angel cards away, but I felt that this lady needed them more than me.

183

An Angel Saved Me

Life went on. I was working hard with my husband and the girls were going to the local school. All was OK, but the shop was not doing well and I kept asking the angels for help. Then one evening the angels came to me and took me to the most fabulous place you have ever seen. I shall try to describe it for you. In my vision I saw willow trees and flowers everywhere. An angel dressed in pure white came to me and brought me to a seat under a willow tree and talked to me. I remember crying and telling him that I did not want to come back down, but he replied that I had to. The following day I was so happy and thankful that I was given the chance to see the angels.

But after my vision the shop went from bad to worse and my husband would not sell it, and as far as my husband was concerned the shop came before his marriage and children. Then in 2006 I became very sick and had to have operations. After six weeks in hospital and two operations we were told that they would have to operate again and it was a fifty-fifty chance if I would make it, so I made a pact with God that if I made it through the operation I would go out and help people who did not make it out of hospital as well as I did. When I came out of hospital my marriage seemed to improve, but it did not take long for the shop to take over our marriage again. Despite this, I just kept thanking my angels for saving me so that I could look after my children.

In 2007 I was offered a job as a home care attendant with the local health department, and I have been working there ever since. Sadly, there was more bad news to come. On 1 March 2010 my husband committed suicide and left me with my two daughters, who are now fourteen and seventeen. I was also left with a shop with more debts than you could ever imagine.

At my husband's funeral the lady I had given the angel cards to all those years ago came up to me and said, 'I think you need these back now.' At that moment I looked up to heaven and knew that my angels would help and comfort me and my two girls in our time of need.

I often wonder what the angels told me about on that wonderful night in heaven, as I could never remember what was said, except that I did not want to come back down. This was very out of character for me as I would not leave my girls for anyone. The last six months have been very hard, and the future is not going to be that easy, but I know that one day we will put this all behind us and the dark tunnel that we are walking through at the moment will be filled with light. I know this because I know my angels are walking with me.

Once again in Cheryl's story we hear about angels giving a person an inner certainty that can keep them feeling safe even when there are clouds on the horizon. There is a sense, an inner strength we are all born with but often fail to recognise, clouded as it often is by doubt, fear and materialism; a sense that we are not alone and, as Adele mentions in her story below, an inner knowing that things will get better and we will be OK.

Amazing!

I had an operation for breast cancer seven years ago. On the night of the operation to remove my lump I woke with a strange feeling. I'm not sure if I dreamed it or not, but I saw an old lady dressed in old-fashioned clothes and with a curly perm. Her feet were not touching the ground and, as I watched her, the most lovely feeling washed all over me. I knew I was going to be OK, and here I am seven years on. I did tell my family about this experience but it didn't make sense until I read your book. Amazing!

I have had more experiences. I lost my mum eighteen months ago. At the time I was scared about going to a hospital for a check-up but on the day of my mammogram the lights on my bedside clock flickered and then I found a big white feather in my car. I took it into work to show everyone. I believe it was my mum telling me things were going to be OK.

In addition to her vision, Adele mentions a big white feather and lights flickering. She believes both to be signs from the other side, which leads us nicely from full-blown angel encounters, or visions, to stories sent in from people who have not seen an angel directly, but have found that meaningful signs or symbols in their daily lives, or unexplained events, have opened them up to the world of spirit.

Let's begin with one of the most common angel calling cards of all – white feathers. Angel signs can be found anywhere and everywhere, but white feathers are perhaps the most well-known signs that the angels are close by. For Rosemarie, Diana and Hilary, whose stories follow on one after the other below, white feathers can be seen to play a significant part in bringing a wonderful sense of unexpected heavenly comfort, purpose and joy.

Firm believer

Last year, 2009 (10 February to be precise), in the middle of the night when my husband and I were both asleep, I heard whispering and 'shuffling' in our bedroom. I couldn't hear what was being said. I was not dreaming, but neither was I fully awake. Some time later I heard a loud bang (as if something had fallen onto the wooden floor) and I woke my husband, who had heard nothing. I took a look around the house and peeped outside just to make sure there was no damage to anything. Perhaps, I thought, something had fallen over. In the morning when I got up, there on the floor next to the bed was a lovely white feather. It was pearly white and silky. I told my husband that we had been visited by an angel.

In September this year, my husband was in hospital for a couple of days. The second night he was in hospital, I recall somebody walking around the bottom of the bed, and the bedding moving as they passed by (just like it occasionally did if my husband went to the loo in the middle of the night and caught the bedding with his hand). I felt the cover being pulled back next to me. I remember thinking, 'Oh! David has come home,' but then, of course, realised he hadn't. I felt his side of the bed go down, the quilt being pulled back over me and what felt like an arm being placed over the top of the quilt to cuddle me. I was definitely awake, but could not open my eyes. They were 'stuck' firmly and I believe whosoever it was came to comfort me but did not want me to see them, because my darling husband died at home a few days later.

It is so very reassuring to know the angels are there to give us comfort in times of adversity and also that other people have had these experiences too. Thank you for reading my story.

Finding feathers

I felt I must write and tell you about an angel happening which occurred last week when we were on holiday. You may recall that I lost my beautiful daughter over two-and-a-half years ago, and ever since then I have found angel feathers and coins from time to time.

My husband and I went on a coach holiday, including a magical day trip to the Lake District. We first had a steam train ride, then a forty-minute boat trip on Windermere where we saw rainbows over the mountains; in fact I have a photo of my husband with a rainbow over his head. Finally, we went to see 'The World of Beatrix Potter'. We had about half an hour to spare before the coach departed and so we went into a little cafe on the pier head. David went to get the tea and something made me glance down. There next to my foot was the most beautiful angel feather. When David came back I said to him, 'Look!' He said, 'Oh, we've got company.' I then picked up the three other feathers.

My late daughter always wanted to visit the Lake District but never managed it and it felt as if she had spent the day with us, which was wonderful. After we came home, we had been out shopping and as I got out of the car at home there were more angel feathers on the ground, as if to say, 'I know you're home and I'm here too.'

I do get so much comfort from finding the feathers. The other part about it is that since early this year I have been struck down by some kind of rheumatoid disease which, as yet, the specialists can't fathom and I'm taking steroids at the moment. After finding the feathers I feel as though I am meant to beat the disease.

The angels continue to be with me. When we were putting up our Christmas decorations I found some small glass angels which a penfriend sent me two years ago. I decided they were too nice and too delicate to be put away all year and so I put them in my china cabinet with other angel items and things my late daughter gave me. You can imagine my surprise when I opened the cabinet to find two angel feathers in there. My husband said I must have put them there and forgotten about it, but I know very well that I didn't.

Learning to fly

I had some amazing experiences yesterday after finishing your book and thinking about guardian angels. I got into the car and immediately a song came on – 'I'm learning to fly, but I ain't got wings'. How bizarre! Later I was sitting in the garden with a cup of coffee enjoying the warm sunshine on my face. A robin started singing its little heart out, followed by a heron flying overhead and then a beautiful dragonfly hovered around me for ages. But then, out of nowhere, a white feather started to drift backwards and forwards a few feet away from me, getting gradually lower until it landed gently on a tub of flowers. I picked it up and held it for a while and felt really calm and happy. This morning, there was another white feather in the middle of the kitchen floor. I was certainly surrounded by angels yesterday!

Both Diane and Hilary mention other common angel signs in their stories – rainbows, birds and songs heard by chance – and these signs also brought feelings of comfort and reassurance. As

I said, there are many ways in which angels and spirits can speak to us. For Emma, it was through another common angel calling card – butterflies – that angels brushed her heart. Here's her experience:

Fluttering

I have just read *An Angel Changed My Life* and felt compelled to write to you.

There have been many dark moments in my life in which I may not have physically seen or felt angels around me, but I instinctively know their hidden strength enabled me to get through these times. My divorce was one of those times. Looking back on it all, I know that I was being guided and supported, though at the time I felt I was so alone. The reason I know for sure is the fact that I am now doing all the things that I once dreamt of and am the strong confident person I never thought I could be. It was a life lesson I was living through back then and one that I had to endure.

The main reason for my writing is to tell you about the time my nana died. She had been poorly for a while and I had visited her in hospital before driving home. When my father phoned to say she had passed, I walked into the kitchen and this beautiful white butterfly flew in from the garden, fluttered around the kitchen, and then flew out of the door. It was almost as if my nana had flown in to say she was now free. It was a very peaceful moment and comforted me greatly. The following week at her funeral tea I looked into her garden and there were two beautiful white butterflies fluttering side by side. Nana had been reunited with my gramps . . . I knew that together they were flying free in spirit. Every time I see a white butterfly – or two – now I know Nana and Gramps are close by saying hello!

Butterflies appear many times in angel stories and it took me a while to realise their close relationship with death, but if you think about it they are the perfect symbol for spiritual rebirth, given their metamorphosis from earthbound caterpillar to beautiful butterfly.

For Margaret, whose enchanting story is next, the medium through which the angels chose to speak to her was fragrance.

Winter roses

Eric was my soul mate and it was hard for me to contemplate life without him. We had been married for twenty-five years. We met when we were both eighteen. I can remember the first time I saw him. We were both invited to a mutual friend's party. I was incredibly shy but this handsome, confident guy just came over and introduced himself. He made me laugh and we talked all evening. When it was time to leave he offered to walk me home.

That walk home was magical. It was snowing but I felt warm inside. Eric told me that the thing he hated most about winter was that the rose-growing season was over. He loved the smell of roses in summer. I can't explain why but it was at that exact moment that I knew I was in love with him. Eight years later we were married. When we moved into our first home one of the first things we did was plant dozens of rose bushes in our garden.

An Angel Saved Me

I can honestly say we had a wonderful marriage; sure, we had our disagreements but the love between us was so strong it could conquer anything. We weren't blessed with children but we were blessed with each other. Losing him after a two-year battle with prostate cancer felt like the end of the world for me. I stopped eating. I stopped going out. I wanted to die. I made a few fragile attempts to step back into life but I missed my Eric so badly I thought I would never be able to go on.

Then one night in the middle of winter I woke up and there was a heavy scent of roses in the air. I got up and went into the garden. There was thick snow covering the rose bushes and the ground was frozen. The scent was definitely coming from inside the house, even though there were no fresh or even dried flowers inside. As I went from room to room the scent seemed to grow stronger. It's hard to describe but I knew Eric was there with me using the scent of roses in winter to take me back to the moment I fell in love with him. He was trying to comfort me. He was sending me a message that I was still living and my life needed to go on. I started to cry because I knew that he wanted me to let go. As I made a silent promise to him to move on the scent vanished.

Although I shall miss Eric deeply until the day I die, the scent of roses that night gave me the strength I needed. It was his way of letting me know that he is watching over me. He had always said if there was a way to reach me after death he would; so he was just keeping his promise.

Other commonly reported heaven-sent fragrances that appear out of nowhere include the scent of vanilla, perfume, bread-baking or any familiar scent that strongly reminds you of a lost loved one. I've also had emails from people who say that feeling a cool breeze on their face when there is no window or door open has been like the touch of an angel. Clocks stopping at significant times after the death of a loved one are likewise well documented, as are lights dimming, bulbs blowing, phones ringing and power surges. All these happenings have been linked to the world of spirit, which is not surprising given that spirit is energy.

Indeed, it could be said that the entire universe is bathed in energy waves that are typically invisible to the human eye: light waves, cosmic waves, gamma rays, X-rays, radio waves, to name but a few. Keeping this in mind, could it be that angels surround us at all times? And just as you can't hear the radio until you switch it on, so you can't see angels or notice the signs of their loving presence unless you tune in emotionally, or are in the zone that allows angels to come through. Many bereaved people have written to me to tell me that it was when they were in a certain emotionally open zone that angels first appeared, often in the form of subtle signs or lights that seemed able to transport them from the depths of sadness to the heights of elation and joy.

It's often the case that not one but a number of subtle angel signs manifest themselves. John feels that he has experienced a number of angel signs and when he puts them all together they are a source of great comfort to him. Here is what he told me.

The day Jennifer died

Jennifer had suffered, since the age of fourteen, from rheumatoid arthritis. Because of her illness, one of her thigh bones had to be frozen, and as a result one leg was 2 ½ inches shorter than the other. Despite this she never complained and refused to register her disability or have any disability allowance. She was always a happy, loving and deeply spiritual being. She died aged sixty-two.

She woke me at four am to say she was going. I was shocked to the core and asked what I could do. She simply asked if I could get her a glass of water as her throat was dry. I did and she drank a full glass. I took the glass back to the bathroom, but was shaking and dropped the glass, smashing it on the floor. Back in bed we snuggled down and she said she felt much better and we fell asleep.

At seven-thirty am I went downstairs and returned to bed with a mug of tea for her at eight a.m. I partly opened the curtains and looked out over the front garden and couldn't believe what I saw. A swirling wind seemed to have flattened plants and several tubs of flowers were, somehow, strewn across the road. The gardens on either side were undisturbed. I left her sitting in bed drinking tea while I popped out to retrieve the flower tubs. I was only gone a couple of minutes. Entering the house I could hear singing; I thought she had put the radio on. I walked upstairs and when I entered her bedroom she lay dead on the floor. I gave her the kiss of life, and the medics came within minutes, but despite all our efforts there was no flicker of life. After half an hour we called it a day. Later I learnt it was an embolism that had worked up her leg and into her lung; there was nothing we could have done. I now realise several things. The singing I heard as I went upstairs was the angels who had come to take her. The plants blown about the garden were a distraction to get me out of the house so I wouldn't see her die and fall to the ground. Her eldest son, who lived six miles away, had refused to go to work that day. Instead, at eight am he went downstairs and sat in a chair. It wasn't until I phoned him at 8.30 am that he understood why he had stayed at home. Her youngest son had also had a strange unsettling morning before I phoned him.

Some two months after she died, I was now living in a flat, feeling quite strange. One night I woke up about one in the morning and saw towards the left-hand side of the bedroom a bright white sphere of light – there were no lights on, nor was there any electrical light in that area. I realised as I watched the intense light that Jennifer had returned to see how I was. I never spoke and after a couple of minutes the light went out, but I remained thrilled and a sense of calm pervaded my body. I still had a long way to go to move on from this sudden loss, but it was a profound moment.

I write this story five years after her death and still the memory is as fresh as though it was only this morning.

Feeling an unexpected sense of emotional well-being, a feeling of being loved and cared for, especially when you are alone – as was the case for John and for Sue whose story follows on next – is, I believe, always the work of your guardian angel.

Something came over me

Mum's in the local hospital now and is likely to be there for a bit – at least until Dad's funeral – so when I'm on my own at night at her house your book will give me comfort. I could stay with my brother and sister-in-law but they're already putting people up for a night or two. I don't feel afraid of being on my own at Mum's, as I know the angels will be all around me.

I feel a lot more positive now. I haven't really thought much about my low-grade non-Hodgkins lymphoma. Something came over me last Friday, as if something had been lifted from me, and it helped me decide that when the time comes for my CT scan and bone marrow biopsy I will get through it all; I will take each day as it comes. I consider myself very fortunate as there are people out there with far more debilitating cancers than mine. I know that with the love and support of good friends and family, of my angels and with a positive attitude I can get through anything. I will keep in touch.

Sue kept her promise to keep in touch and here's the latest email she sent me.

Fantastic news. I went for the results of the bone marrow biopsy and CT scan I had done on 18 November and the scan showed two tiny nodes in my armpit but nothing more. The doctor has part of the bone marrow biopsy back, the fluid part and that's fine; he's just waiting for the bone marrow part which he thinks will be fine too. No one could have given me a better Xmas present. The doctor said I don't need any treatment yet. The blood tests I had done were also fine. I did a dance all down the corridor on the way out (there was nobody about at the time).

Perhaps something similar has happened to you? Life feels hard or you feel sad, and then out of nowhere you get a burst of energy or determination and that pulls you through. That's your angel giving you a hug. Or perhaps you aren't sure what to do next and suddenly you just know which direction you need to head in. Again it's your angel talking to you. And if you get a flutter in your tummy, this might be your guardian angel urging you to follow your gut instinct or intuition. Remember, intuition means knowing something without being aware of how you know it. It is an insight that comes out of nowhere, a sudden knowledge without logical or rational explanation. It is the reassuring, calm and positive voice within you and always one of the simplest but most powerful ways for your guardian angel to communicate with you.

Some people say they hear the voice of an angel or a departed loved one call their name. You may be alone or in a crowded room and you distinctly hear a familiar someone call your name, even though you know that can't be the case. Or, as was the case for Natasha, who sent me another beautiful story below, an angel may call your name and then – when your mind and heart is open – leave other calling cards to inspire and comfort you.

Birthday miracle

On 22 January 2010 it was my twenty-ninth birthday and I was in a happy and contented mood. I had planned to meet up with some friends for a birthday lunch. I decided to go upstairs and wash my hair before meeting with my friends – a girl wants to look her best on her birthday.

I went upstairs and ran a bath. I was home alone that day as my little ones were at school and my husband David was at work. The house was in complete silence and I kind of liked it like that – it had been such a hectic morning and I was enjoying the peace and quiet.

I was in the middle of washing my hair when I heard footsteps downstairs – our house really echoes. I then heard a woman's voice calling out my name several times. I thought it was my mother-in-law, as she had said she would pop round that morning to drop off my birthday presents, so I called back, 'I'm coming, just one minute.' I quickly finished off washing my hair and sorting myself out, and then dashed downstairs to see my mother-in-law.

To my surprise when I got downstairs I found that the house was completely empty. Baffled, I went into the kitchen and turned on the kettle to make a cup of coffee. I remember asking myself if I had imagined someone calling my name – but I knew I hadn't as it had been so clear and I had even heard the footsteps loud and clear.

I was standing in the kitchen playing over in my mind what had just happened when all of a sudden the entire house filled with the most beautiful angelic music. It sounded like a large choir singing right in my dining room.

The music was so very beautiful that I burst into tears and could not stop crying. It seemed to reach down into my very soul and pull at every emotional string I had. It lasted a good few minutes before the house went silent again. The whole kitchen felt warm and had a lovely atmosphere in it.

After that magical experience I just stood there in amazement. I have never heard such beautiful music in all my life. My entire body shook with adrenalin and I felt an overwhelming feeling of inner peace and comfort. For the rest of the day I kept crying – happy and contented tears. It was the most wonderful birthday present I have ever had and one that I will never, ever forget. That magical experience will remain with me for all my life.

As Natasha's story shows, the angels will often send a number of signs your way. There may be one sign that is more significant than others, but frequently a combination of signs occurs – all of them with one purpose in mind and that is to reassure you that you are not alone. This is what happened to Jilly – again it was a number of angel calling cards rather than a single sign that brought her peace of mind.

Love never dies

My beloved husband died five years ago and while he was dying I asked him to let me know that he would be all right on the other side.

A few days after he died I had a power cut. I went to the fusebox and flicked on the electricity again. I then went into the kitchen and

199

found three rings of the cooker on as hot as they can go. The ring that had a ceramic pot on top was cold. This was impossible. That night when I was lying on my bed I felt someone kiss me on the back of my neck – I was the only person in the house. Shortly after this I went to the bathroom in the middle of the night and saw my husband in there as clear as day. I have had several other such experiences but this was the most powerful. I sometimes find myself saying, 'I love you, Jilly,' out of the blue, and once when I was lost I called to him and I heard, 'I am with you always.'

I know that love never dies and I believe in angels. I have angel cards that I consult every day of my life and I know that the angels are always with me.

Another ordinary – but extraordinary – way for angels to reveal themselves is through the magic of coincidences. Here's what Jane has to say:

Support

My mother was recently hospitalised with a stroke and I set about visiting her every day. As I work and have two small children, this took a degree of organisation. There was also my mother's elderly partner, Barry, to consider. He is fairly slow on his feet and although together they are a capable unit I had some anxieties about his ability to cope on his own. Fortunately, a carer named Jackie visits them three times a week for an hour to keep an eye on the situation. Barry, however, is convinced he doesn't really need this support although, as he doesn't drive, it is important.

Last week Barry, my two-year-old son and I had visited my mother in hospital and afterwards I was helping Barry down the path into his home in the dark when I reminded him that Jackie would be coming to visit him the following day to help him go shopping. 'You do know she's coming, don't you?' I said. 'Oh yes,' he insisted.

At this point I heard his home telephone ringing so I ran in to answer it. It was Jackie. 'Hello, I just thought you ought to know that Barry said he doesn't need me to come in this week, but I was a bit worried about it.' At this moment, Barry came into the house and I was able to sort out between them that Jackie would continue to come while my mother was in hospital. I often have the experience when the phone rings that I know who is on the line, but I found the timing of this call extraordinary and it helped to diffuse a potentially difficult situation very effectively. I like to think my guardian angel had a hand in the timing of the call.

Julie's story also features extraordinary events and coincidences and, as she reflects on them, she can clearly recognise the work of her guardian angel.

Extraordinary

The most extraordinary events happened to my little family in the last two days. I had to write to thank you.

My best friend is away for Christmas this year so she gave us our presents early – mine was your book, *An Angel Changed My Life*. Being impatient, I opened it early and started to read your stories. I read how your book often finds its way into people's hands at just the right time in their lives and this was going to be the case for me – although I did not realise it at the time.

I also read the story about an elderly woman saying exactly the right thing to a woman who was contemplating jumping in front of a train and the comfort she had taken from this incident. I was not to know then but by that same evening, I would have an encounter of my own. I have two daughters, and my younger daughter and I were downstairs while my older daughter was upstairs. I am a single mother and sometimes find it hard to play two roles. I had been trying to give my older daughter some guidance and we had ended up arguing, which is why she was upstairs. After a little while, once thing had calmed down I went up and asked her to join us in front of the TV.

After about ten minutes my elder daughter told me the most devastating news: she had taken an overdose of paracetamol. Shock and tears set in. I could hardly hold a clear thought as I gathered my belongings and comforted my daughter while getting my other daughter ready to go to the hospital with us. I was numb.

I went to the hospital choking with fear. Would my daughter die? Was it my fault? Would Social Services take her away?

I explained what had happened to the receptionist and we went and took a seat next to the water dispenser. I looked up through watery eyes and caught sight of an older man, who smiled at me. He was standing right beside me. The room was busy but I heard him say calmly, 'This is not your fault.' I don't know how he knew but it was exactly what I needed to hear.

My daughters and I waited in the room. I did not notice the man any more. Then we went into the doctor, who numbed my daughter's

202

arm and sent us back out to wait for the numbing cream to work before a blood test.

While we were once again sitting there I realised that I had no money to get the car out of the car park. I also knew my bank account was empty, because that same morning we had been to the cash machine and checked it. I had had a balance of nine pounds and we had gone to the shop and bought food with eight of it. The cost to get the car out was two pounds. I could not call my brother because he was abroad for Christmas and so was my best friend and to top it all I had left my mobile phone at home anyway. I thought I might as well try both my debit cards in the hope that one would allow the transaction. I could not believe it because I put a card in and it worked!

Then I realised I had no one to sit with my daughters while I moved the car so I asked the receptionist if she would keep an eye on them and she agreed! I spotted three empty seats in view of the receptionist, and went to move my girls over. When I explained to them that the receptionist was watching them, I turned to point her out. Then I turned back and noticed that the seat next to them was now occupied by the same older man. I felt reassured enough to move the car but when I came back he was gone.

After the blood test we had to wait another hour and a half for the results. She had taken sixteen tablets. My younger daughter was tired and hungry so I suggested we walk to the cash machine next to the food court. I knew I was lucky to have paid for the car and that there was no money, but thought the walk would be good for us because we had been there for five hours. I could not believe my eyes when my account showed fifty pounds. We all had a hot meal.

Eventually, the results came back, and we were told there was paracetamol in my daughter's blood but not enough to cause damage. It was borderline but she needed to see the social worker and doctor in the morning. She was kept overnight. I settled her in hospital, and returned home at five am.

The next day the social workers and doctor interviewed my elder daughter and me. They told us about a girl who had taken seven tablets – my daughter took sixteen – whose brain had swollen, causing her to lose her sight. The social worker was happy for my daughter to come home and concluded she was safe.

We still have counselling to attend and we are all still in shock, but I feel so lucky to have been able to recognise the angel guidance given to us that evening, let alone the provision of money, which had been returned to my account for an overpaid bill. We are not out of the woods yet, but I now know I have, as do my daughters, a guardian angel.

Ruby also believes her guardian angel had a hand in the timing of events that may well have saved her life:

The connection

I'd like to tell you something that happened to me not long after I moved into my bungalow. I needed to have a phone in my bedroom and also internet in another room to connect up to my computer. I was busy banging the pins along the wall and then came to the wardrobe, where I wanted to put the connection. I had a portable landline phone with me and it kept ringing, and every time I answered it there was no reply. When I tried 1471 it told me it did not have the caller's number. I carried on and the phone kept ringing. I thought, this is ridiculous and I'm going to have to phone BT if it carries on. Then I put my hand into the wardrobe and felt an electric wire which fed the socket near the bed which I had not known was there. If I had carried on and the phone hadn't rung when it did, I would have gone straight through the wire and who knows what would have happened.

A telephone also features in this next story sent to me from Pam.

Sorry

I thought you might like to know about my recent experience. I need to tell you the back story first – it is relevant so bear with me.

Gradually in the past few years I have become, I suppose you could say, depressed but functional. My thoughts have been quite dark. I've never got on well with my mother, and a lot of my problems stem from my childhood. She is elderly now and I have had to visit her more often to help out. This has darkened my mood considerably. My sister, who killed herself when I was twelve, has also been in my thoughts. I have been thinking badly of her for taking her own life and leaving me alone to look after Mum.

On the evening of 3 January I was visiting someone during the course of my work when I had cause to use my mobile phone. The screen was a plain white light with the word 'Sorry' in the top left corner. I puzzled out loud, thinking I'd had an incomplete text or had somehow knocked the buttons while the phone was in my pocket. Eventually, the person I was visiting said that I must have a spirit message to apologise for something. I pressed a button on the phone and the message disappeared.

I have tried every button on the phone and can't recreate either the plain white screen or even the font that the word was written in. I know it was a message from my sister as that day was the anniversary of her death. I'm normally quite private about my past but I feel compelled to tell everyone about this.

Of course, you could argue that all the angel calling card stories in this chapter – indeed many in this book – are simply about coincidence, but I believe there is no such thing as coincidence, only the language that angels speak. If you ask your angels to help you or guide you, one of the first ways they are likely to reveal themselves to you is through coincidences, and the more you pay attention to them the more they will occur. So the next time you experience a 'coincidence', rather than dismissing it, ask yourself what it means. The first answer to pop into your mind will often be the truth. The voice in your head will sound like your own – what some may call your intuition – but it is actually the voice of spirit. It will be clear, calm, reassuring and positive. If you hear a second, conflicting and negative answer, then you know it is your fear doing the talking and not your guardian angel.

Many people have written to me to tell me that certain songs speak volumes to them when they 'just happen' to be playing on the radio at exactly the right time, as was the case for Wendy.

Stranger in Paradise

When my grandfather died a few months after my grandmother I was really upset. They had been more like parents than grandparents to me and we were very close. My parents were not around so it was left to me to clear out my grandparents' house. I found it really upsetting and could only manage an hour or two at a time.

One day I was feeling particularly emotional so I decided to have a cup of tea before I got started. I thought it would be a good idea to put on the radio as some music might distract me. I switched on the radio and the song 'Stranger in Paradise' was playing. It's a beautiful song but not at all recent so it was out of the ordinary to hear it playing. But what made it really speak to me was that it was my grandparents' song. They had played it at their wedding. It was very special to them and was popular when they first met. I can remember them playing it and getting all misty-eyed with each other and my grandmother humming it as she did the household chores when I was a little girl. You could say this was just a fabulous coincidence, but for me it was much more than that. It helped dry my tears of sadness and replace them with happy memories. Wherever they are, I'm sure my grandmother and grandfather wanted me to hear it.

Or maybe you catch a snippet of an overheard conversation and what you hear speaks volumes, enlightens or inspires you, or reminds you of something a departed loved one said. Another fascinating way for angels to reveal themselves to us is by the repeated appearance of certain numbers, most commonly the number 11, but as Clare's story shows it does not necessarily have to be the number 11, it could be any combination of numbers that is meaningful to you.

39

My mother died when I was a baby and I have missed her all my life, wondered if it would have been better, easier even, to have some memories of her rather than absolutely none at all. She was beautiful – the photos prove that – but she also was a lovely person on the inside, that's what everyone says.

I've missed her all my life although I've always been convinced she is around, not in a physical sense but in a sense I couldn't quite recognise. When I began reading your book I was immediately reminded of certain incidents, particularly from the last year and a half. I think the last year has been a catalyst for me in the sense that I have become more peaceful with myself, started to have some self-love, stopped caring so much what others think, and learnt to appreciate that I'm all right – in fact I'm pretty good!

A lot of things have happened to me but this is quite unusual. Around six months ago I was lying in bed one night and the usual things were floating around in my head. I started thinking about my mum. I was in a very restful state probably not far from sleep. I was thinking to myself, 'What age was Mummy when she died? I know she was 39 but what age exactly? Well, her birthday was on 24 May and she died 1 December so that's 39 years, 6 months and 8 days.' Then I thought to myself that that was a bit mad, why would I think something like that, it had never entered my head before, and I fell asleep.

The next day I got up and remembered my thoughts from the night before. I wondered what age I was, and doing some sums in my head I realised I was exactly 39 years, 6 months and 8 days. There was only ever going to be one day in my life that I would be the exact same age as my mother was when she died!

There are also stories of people who find themselves inexplicably drawn towards buying a newspaper, magazine or book they would not ordinarily buy and then finding that there is a story or report in it that is perfectly relevant to them. Quite a few people now have written to me to tell me that one of my angel books appeared at just the right time to heal or encourage them. Here's what Amanda told me:

Angel friends

This morning I finished reading your book *How to See Your Angels* and the most amazing thing has happened, so I really feel inspired to abandon all chores and email you pronto.

I am an artist (only part-time) and I have been thinking about setting up a website because my work has dried up. At present I operate on a word-of-mouth basis. As I put down your book I sent out a thought to the angels to help me. I remember saying (in my head), 'Please send me some orders, I am not asking for something for nothing because I am prepared to put the work in.' As you are probably aware, painting is an exacting and lengthy occupation.

I took myself off into the conservatory to have a cigarette (I know, it's a filthy habit) and while I was smoking (only minutes after

I put down your book) the telephone rang. It was my husband telling me that someone had just asked him to ask me if I could paint someone's pet dog and also a portrait of two children. It seems that they are going to be Christmas presents.

As I said, at present I only work by word of mouth so how amazing is that?! My husband had only popped into the hairdressers. All this has happened in the last forty-five minutes . . . I'm so shocked I'll have to get myself another cigarette to calm myself down! Thank you, my angel friends. Thank you so much. I have always believed in angels because I remember seeing them circling my bedroom ceiling when I was a little girl, but to my mind this is incredible.

I know that this story sounds bizarre but I swear on my life that it has really happened.

Samantha sent me this email.

Angels all around

I have just completed your book *An Angel Changed My Life*, and it was such fantastic reading, I found it impossible to put the book down until I had finished it.

The reason that I want to extend my thanks to you is that I have known about angels being around me since I was a very young girl. I have had many, many experiences that could be construed as psychic; however, after reading your book I actually believe that angels have been stepping in along the way to help me. This realisation has really made me see that I am very blessed to be touched by angels, and that I have so much more to give.

210

I have always wanted to be a writer, but never really had that extra push to do it, but after thinking about it, I am going to start my writing by going through all the experiences that I have had. I hope one day to be published, so that others can share my experiences. If it had not been for your book then I would probably have just carried on dreaming about writing, so again, thank you so very much.

Fabien also believes he was meant to read an angel book:

Your book

I bought your book *An Angel Changed My Life* yesterday and saw your email address (I was surprised that it could be so easy to write to you.) I bought your book because Jacqueline, the love of my life, was reading it and when she finished it in May she told me, 'You must read it, you will like it a lot.' She knows exactly what I like to read.

Last June she had a brain haemorrhage and today she is in the Royal Hospital for Neuro-disability in Putney, London. A week ago, when she was moved there from Peterborough where we lived, the hospital asked me to bring some of her personal stuff. And when I took some books, one fell on the floor and it was yours . . .

Yesterday, as I was coming from the hospital to Notting Hill to meet my nephew, he texted me to say he was going to be late, so I went into a WHSmith and there in front of me was your book again, so I bought it.

I don't know what all this means, but I believe in coincidences, and am receiving many incredible insights.

Perhaps you've read a book that changed your life or a poem that spoke directly to your heart, or perhaps you heard a piece of music and for a brief moment you caught a glimpse of the other side. Your angels can and do use all these media to inspire you.

One book that contains many gems of life-altering advice and found its way into my hands at just the right moment in my life is *The Power of Now* by Eckhart Tolle. The book's message is simple but profound: living in the now is the truest path to happiness and spiritual awakening. The book explains how destructive patterns of negative thinking and fear can confound one's spiritual and even physical well-being, and shows how these patterns can be dissolved. A perfect partner for this book is *The Secret* by Rhonda Byrne, a modern bible for positive thinking and living. Then there is M. Scott Peck's *The Road Less Travelled*. If you haven't read this book yet I urge you to do so. I certainly wish someone had recommended it to me in my teens or twenties. Peck shatters the myth that life is meant to be easy and explains the importance of challenge and struggle and of delaying gratification for spiritual growth, as well as accepting responsibility for decisions made and dedicating oneself to truth.

Poetry is another beautiful medium that angels like to use to bring us closer to the truth. I have been inspired all my life by the evergreen beauty of the words in *The Desiderata* ('Go placidly amid the noise and haste ...') as well as Mary Frye's haunting 'Do not stand at my grave and weep'. And don't get me started on music and its ability to take us to another time and place and lift our spirit to great heights. There are so many heaven-sent pieces of music I could wax lyrical about, but there will always a special place in my heart for *Miserere Mei, Deus* – if you've never heard this choral piece you're missing out on something very special. It's incredibly inspiring and uplifting. And never underestimate the power of a good movie to inspire or motivate you. I've already mentioned *The Shawshank Redemption*, but another movie that never fails to raise my spirits is *Coach Carter*. But I'm sure that I don't really need to guide you to music, words, films or art that can lift and inspire you, because all your life your angels have already been doing that for you. So the next time you feel moved or uplifted in some way by a book, poem, song or work of art, let your spirit drink it all in.

Others say they hear answers to their heartfelt questions when they use the radio, TV or internet or they see the answer on a sticker on a window, bus or cab or even a message on someone's T-shirt. Another sign I urge you to notice is a high-pitched ringing in the ear that stays for a very short while and then fades away, or the feeling that someone is standing behind you but when you turn around there is no one there. Whenever you get either of these sensations, use them as opportunities to relax, shut your eyes and take a moment to count your blessings and thank your guardian angel for being there.

And don't forget about the power of humour to bring you closer to heaven. Remember that famous Chesterton quote – 'Angels can fly because they take themselves lightly.' Seriousness of purpose and humour can go together. Sadly, many religious services and spiritual events today are completely devoid of humour, as if laughter and heaven don't mix, but this couldn't be further from the truth. Your angels fly close to you every time you smile, laugh or have fun – as long as it is good-natured fun, so don't ever hold back when it comes to laughter. I think this next charming story, sent to me by Sara, illustrates my point well.

Laughter in heaven

When my husband died one of the things I missed most about him was his warm sense of humour. He was one of those guys who laughed his way through life and I needed that because I tend to be on the serious side. He died five years ago and I took it badly. I missed him so much, but what pulled me through was the love of my children. They were only fifteen and seventeen at the time and they needed me to be there for them. My youngest left for college this year, though, and I felt really alone and low again.

One Sunday morning I woke up feeling so very sad. I cried and cried and missed my husband so much. I thought about the last five years without him and how sombre things had been for me. I decided to go to church as usual, hoping this would help, but it actually made me feel worse as I remembered all the times I had gone to church with my husband. Now I was going alone. I would have given anything for a sign from him that he was still close by.

I got that sign in the most unexpected way and this is what happened. The service was well under way and we had sung a few hymns and now it was time for the first reading. The vicar stood up and looked a bit uncertain but started to read the story of Mary

Magdalene washing Jesus's feet. As he read I could see him squinting and standing as far back from the text as possible. It was obvious to me that he had forgotten his spectacles and I could feel myself smiling inside as I often forget my spectacles. There was more to come because I then heard him confidently inform the congregation that Mary washed Jesus's hair with her feet. I looked at the woman beside me and like two giggling schoolgirls we could not stop ourselves laughing until we cried. The poor vicar tried to carry on but most of the congregation was chortling by now.

It felt so good to laugh again and it was only later that I realised this was the sign from my husband I had longed for. He wanted me to have fun again.

Angels may also leave items of value for you to find. These may be lost items that mean a great deal suddenly appearing at just the right moment, or coins found in unusual places, again at just the right moment. Jackie's story illustrates this well.

Housework

Reading your book inspired me to share a story with you. It was something that happened to me a few years ago. I used to do housework for an elderly gentleman whom I will call Lenny; I also used to do the same for a couple a few doors up the street in a house with the same layout as Lenny's.

Lenny had always had a fear of dying and death and refused to go to the funerals of his friends who had passed over. One day when I was vacuuming in the hallway at Lenny's I noticed a pound coin up

215

against the skirting board. I picked it up, handed it to Lenny and thought no more about it.

A few months later Lenny became ill and died in hospital. A week or so after his funeral I was vacuuming the stairs of the couple up the street from Lenny's house when I remembered how scared Lenny had been of dying and death. I said to myself, 'If you are OK, Lenny, please give me a sign,' and then I carried on with my work. When I reached the bottom step something caught my eye and there up against the skirting board in exactly the same place as the one that I had found in Lenny's house was a pound coin. I felt a tingle from the top of my head right down through my body as I remembered the pound coin I had found in Lenny's house. I felt sure that this was my sign.

Rest assured, your angels will always try to communicate with you and they will use any number of subtle signs to get your attention. And when you do start noticing their signs and allow yourself to be guided by them you may just find that everything in your life starts to come together at last, as it did for Mandy.

How cool is that!

Reading all the stories in your book resonated with my many experiences of dreams, visions, connection with those who have passed over and so on, and brought angels to the forefront of my daily life in a more conscious way, opening a dialogue, if you like. My angels are answering loud and clear already. At work the other day the colleague I share a room with had a big problem and was really stressed. I asked the angels to help him and literally one minute later a package was brought to me by the receptionist that solved his problem; an immediate sign that angels were in the room.

Today, I went to the passport office to apply for a second passport because I live in two countries and travel back and forth and have recently become involved with an overseas charity project in a country that needs a visa and ties up my passport. I was worried they would not grant me the second one because it is usually only allowed for paid work. But the man was open to the idea that work included volunteer work and luckily he gave me the new passport. When I looked at the photo I saw that the security hologram over it looked like a pair of angel wings. How cool is that!

The more you notice the magic and wonder in your daily life the more angels will become an everyday reality for you. Meaningful coincidences, feathers and dreams are fairly common but, as I never tire of repeating, angels don't restrict themselves in any way. You can see your angels anywhere and everywhere, from birdsong to clouds, from rainbows to lost objects found, from sunshine to rain, from tears to laughter and in every act of kindness and every loving thought. Their presence can be felt in every atom of creation. They are part of that very real interconnection between all things visible and invisible.

One truth

All the moments of enchantment in this chapter convinced the person who experienced them of one truth and one reality – that we are spiritual beings in human form. The clouds of materialism and scepticism melted away, enabling them to catch a glimpse of an 'unnamed something' that held them safe. Maybe there has been a similar moment in your life when the truth dawned on you? Remember, if you don't think you have encountered angels, many of the people here didn't actually see angels. Something as simple as a feather, a song, a book, a flash of intuition or a remarkable coincidence was the catalyst for their spiritual transformation. If you look at the world with 'angel eyes', every moment is a chance for you to glimpse the mystery and to marvel at the sheer magic of it all.

Hopefully, by now you may be close to accepting that many strange and wonderful things can and do happen in life, and if something happens, it is possible. If you're still thinking that some of these experiences are down to chance or coincidence, remember that coincidence is the language that angels speak.

And perhaps now as we draw towards the end of this book you are ready to accept and embrace stories of angels in human form ...

CHAPTER SEVEN

Touched by an Angel

An angel is someone who helps you believe in miracles again.

Author unknown

Anyone can be an angel.

Author unknown

Angels can become visible when necessary, but our ability to sense and see them ordinarily is limited in much the same way as we cannot see the structure of atoms or the flow of electricity or sound waves. However, as you've seen in some of the stories so far, there are instances when visions of all-embracing love can and do reveal themselves. Sometimes these visions can take the traditional form of blinding light, wings and halos, but there are also examples of angels manifesting themselves in a human form. This chapter is all about angels revealing themselves through the words and deeds of ordinary people, consciously or unconsciously guided from above. And let's start at the very beginning with some stories about children.

Little angels

Angelic encounters of all kinds, whether in human or divine form, are more likely to happen in childhood because a child is more natural, spontaneous and willing to suspend disbelief than an adult. If you ever need a shot in the arm to believe in angels, talk to children about them. Fresh from heaven, there is a special connection between children and the world of spirit, so let's begin with some child-focused stories. Reading them really can offer a glimpse of the divine manifesting in human form.

Children can teach us so much more about spiritual growth than we can ever teach them, and nowhere is this truer than in their attitude towards dying and death. As this next, breath-takingly moving story sent to me by Nicole shows, they simply don't believe in it. I cry every time I read this story and I have read it many times.

Living in the presence of an angel

I believe that I have been living in the presence of an angel for the past nine years, and it is only now that he has returned to heaven that I have realised this to be so. My darling little angel is called Charlie. He lost his life on 5 June 2010, aged just eight and a half years, from anaphylactic shock.

Charlie was born on 27 November 2001 and right from the start my dad used to say, 'Where has this child come from?' He recognised something extraordinarily special about him from the moment he was born. Everyone used to comment on his 'knowing eyes' even

220

when he was a tiny baby. I, however, was just plain exhausted since Charlie was a very colicky baby and the sleepless nights went on for many months. I did not begin to see his special qualities until he reached about a year old and his sleep improved.

I suppose to my embarrassment I would describe myself then as being a bit of a smug mum, although I hoped I kept my smugness to myself. Charlie was always so exceptionally well-behaved and obedient; I can honestly say he never had a toddler tantrum! I used to think it was all down to our perfect parenting skills. However, after the subsequent arrival of two 'spirited' siblings for Charlie – my daughter Izzy in 2004 and son Samuel in 2007 – I had a rapid re-think. I came to recognise that Charlie was innately special, and that it had little to do with how we had brought him up. He would have been good whatever his upbringing.

Over the following years Charlie developed into a lovely young boy. He was the most loving and caring big brother. I remember how up until his death a few months ago, Charlie would take a restless Samuel into his own bed at night so as not to disturb our sleep. I had to tell Charlie on many occasions that it was our job to look after Samuel at night, that he had school to get up for, but to no avail. Of a morning I would regularly find the two boys snuggled up in Charlie's bed.

There was something truly exceptional about Charlie. He never complained about his medical conditions, yet he had severe food allergies, coupled with asthma and hay fever. He lived with a life-threatening condition every day, yet it wasn't who he was. He was a bright, much-loved, energetic little boy with a zeal for life, who had friends in abundance. I would marvel daily at why I had been blessed

221

with such a wonderful, caring and helpful child. My life was nothing short of perfect.

I could go on and on all day about Charlie; he was everything to us and he has left a huge void in our lives and those around us. He has touched the hearts of people the world over who remember our precious son and his 'sunny' ways. He has created a legacy that lives on despite his passing. People in the community regularly stop me in the street to recall a special memory about Charlie, often involving the kindness he showed to their own children.

It is only now that he has gone that I have come to realise what he is and always was. I am not a religious person, but the strangest transformation has happened in my life since he has been gone. It is as though my eyes have been opened to a whole new way of life, a spiritual world that I never knew existed. I now truly believe my little boy was a gift from heaven sent to bring joy to us and the world around him. Heaven loaned us this beautiful child and he has now returned to the place he came from – heaven. It is only now in his passing that we have come to realise we were living in the presence of an angel and continue to do so.

I have had many signs that Charlie is still very much part of our lives. I have collected twenty white feathers (Charlie has been gone almost twenty weeks) found in the most unusual places about the house and those that have landed in my hair or at my feet when I have been at my lowest and in need of reassurance. I have felt Charlie's presence very strongly, especially in his bedroom where his little brother Samuel continues to sleep. On two occasions now I have slept in Charlie's bed to help Samuel settle. Both times I have felt the pressure of small feet standing on my legs beneath the duvet when I have been sleeping. This has made me wake with a start, fully expecting to see Samuel on the end of the bed. However. on both occasions, Samuel has been tucked up in his own bed, sound asleep. On returning to bed the first time this happened, I saw a perfectly white little feather glistening by the pillow (the pillows are hollow fibre) and on the second time I found one tucked in the corner of the bedroom. This didn't surprise me as I felt Charlie's presence strongly. My family, close friends and I have also been visited daily by robins since the day Charlie died. We have had some quite amazing experiences with robins, and believe these to be visits from Charlie in spirit form.

I feel privileged to have had Charlie in my life and thank heaven for blessing us with him even for such a short while. I can in all honesty say that if we were offered that time again with him I would take it in an instant, even with the same devastating outcome.

Since Charlie's passing I have met with a group of mums who have recently lost their young boys in similar and tragic circumstances. On talking with these mums, we learned an unusual thing – that all of our boys shared too many personality traits for it to be coincidence. They were the eldest in the family and were very different from their younger siblings. They were mature and 'wise' beyond their years, almost like having a third adult in the house, and could hold very in-depth conversations despite their tender years. All of the boys lived life at top speed, throwing themselves into all activities, be it football, golf, sailing, Cubs, swimming, with a passion. They never did anything in half measures; it was almost as though they sensed they had so little time on earth to fit everything in. They were all exceptionally bright boys too, high achievers at school. Everything they did they seemed to excel at. Above all, though, our boys were blessed with the kindest hearts. They were generous with their time and love for everyone around them and were always compassionate towards those less able than themselves. They were truly angelic and inspiring.

I wonder if during your research into angels you have come across similar findings about children who have passed over? I seem to read over and over again in newspaper reports and books about children who have died being described in very similar ways. It seems to be a common link between these children. It is as though they have been hand-picked by heaven to return to its care when they have learnt all of life's lessons necessary to mature their souls. Maybe this is why we always felt that Charlie had an 'old soul' in a young body. His soul was more than ready to return, although his body was physically immature.

I wrote back to Nicole to tell her I agreed wholeheartedly. Children like Charlie are incredibly special and perhaps the closest thing to an angel on earth. Their time on earth is brief but the imprint they leave on the hearts of those who love them never fades.

Of course, not all children will display the same remarkable courage and spirituality as Charlie did, but within each of them there is always that potential. Indeed many people, myself included, believe that children are little angels in human form sent to guide and inspire us.

Debs sent me this story about her two-year-old son.

Misty light

I have just read your lovely book and would like to tell you my experience. It was about twelve years ago and, without telling anyone, I had been trying to meditate with angels. When I had finished I came out of my bedroom and my two-year-old son looked at me and said, 'Mummy, have you been talking with the angels?'

Some time later I woke up in the night and saw an angel floating alongside my bed. His head was at the bottom end and his feet at the top. I could see wings tucked under him, gently rising and falling beside me. I turned over and closed my eyes, turned back and he was still there. I did this a few times. He had a long robe and there was a misty light around him which lit up the bedroom. I just lay watching him until I fell asleep.

Like Debs, Emma is convinced that her child's openness to the spirit world is strengthening her own connection with the angels.

Little signs

I seem to be getting more little signs that my angels are near. I think the reason is my daughter. She is so alert for a just-turned-one year old. There is definitely something special about her. When she is babbling away, I sense there is someone visiting. I'm getting more and more used to it as it is happening more and more often. I don't get as freaked out as I used to, and I encourage her and ask her who is there to see her. I think it's getting more frequent as she is getting even more active and she has just started walking. It is so intriguing and just makes me fascinated to learn more about the unknown.

As I said, children can teach us a great deal about the world of spirit and all of us, whether we have children in our lives or not, can reclaim the unquestioning openness of children's minds that helps them see what adults often can't. All of us can grow spiritually by reconnecting with the little child that still lives within us, the part of us through which our guardian angel speaks.

Children seem to accept angelic encounters with far more equanimity than adults, perhaps because they have not yet experienced a clear division between this world and the next and are therefore, for a little while, a part of each. Sadly, as children grow older many lose their innate spirituality when they acquire greater knowledge and an unwillingness to take things at face value any more. The acquisition of knowledge as we age is not necessarily a negative thing, but it can work against nurturing childlike qualities of open-mindedness, enthusiasm, trust and emotional spontaneity that draw angels nearer to us. It is, however, possible to grow older in years without losing touch with the child in our heart. It is possible to stay young in spirit and reclaim our special bond with heaven – a bond that is our birthright.

One way or another

Children are more likely than adults to encounter angels, but evidence suggests that when aid is needed celestial helpers can manifest to anyone, whatever age they may be. They can also appear in any shape or form and — forgive me for digressing a little from the angels-in-human-form theme in this chapter, but I do want to mention another common way for heaven to reveal itself on earth — is through pets.

Every day all over the world pets are comforting, protecting and offering their owners unconditional love and devotion. I've read countless stories of pets brightening the lives of those who care for them and this one below sent to me by Elizabeth is a fine example:

My friend

I just feel I want to tell you my story about my cat so you can understand how I feel about losing him.

It was last year when everything that I had been holding inside me for years came to a head. Last May I tried to commit suicide because I felt I couldn't get over the past and I had very low self-esteem, no confidence and hated myself. I ended up in hospital the day I took the overdose. My mum was heartbroken but understands it was my way of saying I couldn't cope.

Anyway, not long after this, I was still very down and my boyfriend and I noticed a wee stray cat coming round. His coat was dull and you could just tell he wasn't getting looked after so I thought he was living on the streets. When we first approached him he was very vicious — I suppose being protective of himself — so I just kept feeding him and eventually he started to come closer to me. After a couple weeks I sat with the back door open and he came in for the first time, so I got up and fed him, then tut-tutted and he came over to me on the sofa and curled up on my knee. It was lovely for him to do that because I felt that he trusted me and knew I would never hurt him.

Eventually he moved in full-time. He was my wee follower — everywhere I went, he was there — and our bond grew. Every night when I went to bed he would jump off the sofa and come to bed with me. Over the year we had him it was lovely to watch the change in him from hissing and scratching and biting to purring and giving his love back to us.

Unfortunately he took ill on Tuesday, 26 October 2010, and died a few days later. I wailed and sobbed. It was as if someone had ripped my heart out. I believe my cat came to me in my time of need and healing. He helped me through my depression and I helped him have a good last year of his life. I will never forget my wee man. He is in my heart safely locked away and there he will stay.

Becki believes her beloved pet not only brought healing but may well have saved her life.

Archie

It's one of those things that's easy to put down to coincidence, but for me I know it's true. In November of 2009 I took a trip to Devon (I live in Kent) and saw an advert for some kittens. I was only in Devon for twenty-four hours so to add another seventy miles onto my journey was crazy! I'd never had a cat before, had never even been very keen on them, but in a moment of madness I drove all the way in the pouring rain for a beautiful little ginger tom.

Touched by an Angel

I'd intended to buy two kittens (in for a penny, in for a pound, eh?!) and I wanted two females but when I got there this little ginger tom stole my heart. When I got him home he was just wonderful. I had a sixteen-year-old cocker spaniel who had just come out of surgery; my little cat (now named Archie) would climb on top of him when he was sick, and purr to him until he woke up. I can't explain it, but you could just tell he knew the dog was sick and wanted to be nice to him.

As time went on Archie became a prolific hunter. At six months old I had decided to let him explore the outdoors (well, I didn't really decide – he kept bolting out of the door and driving me mad at two am trying to get in, until I got him a catflap!). He brought me gifts every day after my spaniel passed away – he was so in tune with how I was feeling. Dead mice and rabbits weren't exactly what I'd hoped for, I must admit.

Sadly in July of this year he was killed by a fox. It is still incredibly painful for me. He had tried to get home but had bled to death close to his favourite tree. I think maybe he had been stalking some cubs, and the mother had tried to protect them.

Over the months he was in my life, I had been feeling increasingly unwell, but just never got around to going to the doctor. I just hate those places, and had almost convinced myself I just felt horrible from stress. A few weeks after my sweet Archie died I had such a vivid dream about him and he told me I needed to go to the doctor that day. Well, I'm a little superstitious so I did as he told me, and thank God I did. By the time I got to the GP I was so sick that I was immediately rushed to A&E and diagnosed with type 1 diabetes that was so out of control I was no more than an day away from going into a coma. My organs had already begun to shut down.

I can't see why such a beautiful soul as Archie was taken in such a pointless act – but I really do wonder what would have happened to me if he hadn't died and come through to me in a dream. I think he probably saved my life.

Whenever there is love, there is healing. There is also no death as these next two stories show. The first comes from Cecily:

Wonderful memories

In the winter of 2004 I had a virus and was very depressed and then I slowly began to fall very ill with ME. I was in agony for most of the day and so tired sometimes opening my eyes was a strain.

Unable to work, I spent a lot of time on my own at home and for reasons I can't understand my thoughts kept returning to my dog, Chloe. She had died over twenty years before. She had been a present for me when I was eight years old and we had been inseparable. I loved her passionately and she was the most devoted dog in the world. It broke my heart when she died. Then one night I fell asleep and half woke up to hear Chloe's familiar barking. It was so real I thought she had to be in the room with me, but then I woke up a little more and realised it was just a dream.

I fell asleep again and had the most incredible dream. In my dream I was walking in a beautiful wood and standing close by were my brother and Chloe. As soon as Chloe saw me she came rushing over. We had the most wonderful cuddle. I told her how much I missed her. Then Chloe started to race back towards the woods. I tried to follow her but my brother stopped me and said, 'No,' and then I woke up.

I sat there in bed crying for a while but I also knew that I needed to get better and get my life back again. I had wonderful memories of my Chloe and they were like a spur to me to move on – they really gave me strength. But this isn't the most incredible part of my story. The next morning my brother called around with a gift for me and, would you believe it, it was a puppy just like Chloe. Now there is another dog saving my life.

And this one comes from Amy.

Long lives

My last cats were called Kitty and Weasel – they were mother and daughter. Weasel had a litter of kittens and my son, who was a little boy then, wanted to keep one of them whom we named Kitty. Both were black with a white chest and white paws. They both had very long lives. Weasel was sixteen when she passed away and Kitty was twenty!

They were wonderful cats and always used to curl up on my bed with me when I wasn't well. They had very expressive meows; each cat's was different. I am sure they used to talk to me! The day after Kitty passed away I woke up in the morning and heard this really loud purring in my ear! I am sure she was saying goodbye and telling me she was safe.

I've had many stories sent to me over the years about beloved cats and dogs as well as other pets, including rabbits, mice, ferrets, parrots and horses, returning to their owners in spirit form for one last goodbye. There are some who say that animals cannot return in spirit form because they have no soul but wherever there is love, there is spirit, and there is no separation. With their selfless devotion, love and companionship, pets sound a lot like angels to me.

Earth angels

Saved by an angel? Let me count the ways.

There is a belief that we all see or experience the presence of angels in one form or another. Many times they come into our lives and we don't recognise them for what they are, and this is especially the case when angels manifest their loving presence through the words and actions of other people or, as I call them, earth angels.

Angels can work their magic on earth not only through children and animals but through other people. Regardless of whether or not these people know they are being guided by a higher power, to me they are earth angels. In Fiona's mind there is no doubt an earth angel saved her granddaughter's life. Here's her striking story.

Swept away

Five years ago I took my toddler granddaughter with me on a shopping trip. We had a great time but after a couple of hours she started to get tired and cranky so I decided it was time to go home. We went back to my car and I asked her to stand still while I loaded the bags into the boot. I was in the middle of lifting the first bag when I saw her shoot off down the pavement. I've got hip problems so I could not race after her. I called out to her because I was terrified she would run into the oncoming traffic. It was such a busy road. She didn't seem to hear me and my heart stopped when I saw her close to the kerb. She was just about to step off into the road when this elderly lady – I mean she was older than me because she had grey hair – appeared out of nowhere and scooped her up in her arms.

When I got there the lady put my granddaughter down and I immediately bent down and started to tell her off. Then I remembered I had not thanked the old lady, but when I stood up she had just gone. I mean she was nowhere. I don't know how an old lady could have got away so fast without me at least seeing her in the distance. To this day I still don't know how she appeared and disappeared in such a busy, open area. I believe she was an angel sent to save my granddaughter.

Was the lady who saved Fiona's granddaughter's life an angel? Her mysterious appearance at just the right time and the way in which she vanished afterwards appear to suggest that she was.

There's nothing ordinary or easily explainable about this next encounter either, sent to me by Evie.

No broken bones

I was out hillwalking in the Lake District and I was trying to jump across a stream. It was stupid really as I could easily have walked over the bridge, but anyway I tried to jump and fell into the water. It

233

was freezing cold and deeper than I thought, coming right up to my shoulders. I felt this sharp pain in my right ankle and was convinced it was broken. I tried to climb out but the pain was unbearable. Eventually, I managed to hop to the other side but when I tried to pull myself out, the mud on the banks kept slipping under my hands. I couldn't get out and night was beginning to fall. I knew I was in serious trouble. I tried to get into my rucksack to reach my mobile phone, but when I eventually got it out I had no signal. All I could do was stand and wait for other walkers. I called out but heard only my own voice echoing back to me.

After an hour or so, my face and hands felt numb with cold. It was getting very dark. I tried one more time to get out but could barely move a muscle; I had never felt so tired and this overwhelming urge to fall asleep came over me. All I wanted to do was shut my eyes, but then I heard this voice telling me to keep my eyes open. I looked around me and standing over me was this man in a white coat. He had really large black eyes. He held out his hand and urged me to grab it. Giddy with exhaustion and happiness, I took hold of his hand and as I did I felt a surge of warmth go through my body. I'm not joking. I didn't feel cold any more.

When he had got me out he told me to lean on him and he would get me to a safe place. I told him I couldn't walk because I had broken my ankle. He looked at me and told me I had no broken bones, just a strain. I don't know how he could tell that because it was pitch dark by now. Anyway, I leaned on him and we started to walk together. I asked him who he was and he said he had been sent to help me and one day I would see him again. I was too tired and hungry to ask any more questions. After about ten minutes of walking – or in my case hobbling – we reached a pub and the man helped me to the door. I hobbled over to the bar and asked for an ambulance to be called. I told the bartender where I had fallen and how this man had helped me. The bartender asked, 'What man?' but when I turned around to point him out he had gone.

My story gets even more amazing when I tell you that the doctors found no broken bones in my ankle, just torn ligaments. The bartender told me that if I had fallen in the place I told him I did it would take at least an hour to walk back to the pub, but it took us about ten minutes.

I told some of my friends about my encounter and many of them agree with me that heaven sent an angel appropriately dressed in a white coat to save me.

I've read enough stories over the years to know that angels can and do watch over us in the guise of ordinary people. I'm also convinced that sometimes they place people in our lives to give us encouragement, love and hope at just the time when we need it the most. Linda's story demonstrates the awesome power of a few well-chosen words during a moment of crisis.

Whole again

After a two-year engagement my boyfriend broke up with me. There was no explanation, no warning. One day we were a couple, the next he had moved out. I still don't understand it to this day. I'd never had much self-confidence so my boyfriend walking out on me like that got me questioning everything about myself. Within a month I was in a real state. I hated the way I looked; I hated everything about me. I started to go out with a guy who didn't treat me very well. He was rough and rude, but a part of me felt like that was all I deserved. Gosh, I had such low self-esteem. It makes me cry now to think I was once like that. I longed to be in a happy relationship but the harder I tried, the worse things got.

The day my life changed for the better started much like any other. I went to work as usual. I was unhappy and feeling low, as ever. In a week's time I would be thirty-five. All my friends were married and some had kids. I didn't have anyone. All during the day at work I felt myself welling up and I had to escape to the restrooms to have a good cry. My life seemed to be heading nowhere. It was while I was in the toilet having a good cry that I heard someone else come in. I dried my eyes, went out of the cubicle and started to wash my hands. This lady stood next to me and started to comb her hair. She was really beautiful. She had such long blonde hair. I took one look at her and then at myself in the mirror and it got too much. I lost control and started to sob and sob.

The lady didn't say anything; she just held me and let me cry on her shoulder. Eventually she asked me what was wrong and I told her all about my boyfriend woes and how I seemed to attract all the wrong men. She wiped the tears from my eyes and said something really simple but incredible. She said, 'I don't know if this will help or not, but when my marriage ended and I thought I would never find anyone again my grandmother told me that I should try to become the person I wanted to marry. It really helped me.' Then she smiled and walked out.

I stood there and thought about what this lovely lady had told me. Suddenly it made sense. What was I missing? Could I be that person for myself? I wanted a man who was intelligent, attractive and had a sense of humour. When I was at school I used to have all those qualities. It was time to find them again.

As I said, it was the most simple but beautiful advice. It really turned my life around. I don't know who that lady was, and nobody in the office could place her either, but she was an angel for me because she said something to me that made perfect sense. I was looking outside of myself for all the qualities that I thought would make me whole, when the place I should have been looking for them was within. Since that day I've gone back to college, got a promotion and moved out of my parents' house. I'm still single but I'm single and loving it, which has made a huge difference. I don't wake up feeling like half a person any more.

Was the blonde stranger just a caring, kind person? If so, then why did no one see her in the office before or since? She was very beautiful and surely someone would have noticed her. This story has all the hallmarks of a guardian angel story – the kind helpful person who appears at just the right time in your life. Linda told me also how comforted and relieved the woman made her feel – even though she had never met her before.

Sure, angels can and do appear in their celestial form, but far more common and in my mind just as uplifting and awesome are angels who manifest themselves in human form. They may not arrive with a blast of trumpets but they are angels all the same. And one of the least recognised earth angels is the one that can manifest within us when we need it the most. Here's what Rebecca told me.

Give me strength

I was on a night out with my friends but after an unpleasant incident involving another woman I was asked to leave the club. My friends were inside the club and had my money and I was upset and just wanted to get home. The door staff wouldn't let me back in, not even to get my money, so it looked like I would have to walk the few miles home.

A man came out of the nightclub and kept asking if I was OK and said he would run me home. I refused at first, but after he offered a few more times I agreed (as I thought it would be safer than walking late at night) and I just wanted to get home to my boyfriend. We set off towards his car and we seemed to be walking for ages. Little did I know at the time that he had no intention of driving me home.

We arrived at this house and I saw a car in the drive and was relieved so I sat on the bonnet as he nipped into the house. When he came out the next thing I remember is being thrown backwards onto the bonnet and he was trying to rape me. I screamed and he put his hand over my mouth hard. He was so strong and I was pinned down on the bonnet, but at that moment I got such a surge of strength that I managed to throw him off me and stop the rape. I ran straight out into the main road and a car stopped for me. It was a young man, and he was none other than an off-duty police officer! He could clearly see I was distressed. I told him I was being attacked and he took me straight to a public place and rang the police. The police got my attacker that night.

The more I've reflected on the events of that night the more I know that an angel actually saved my life. My attacker was a big strong young male and I am a very petite young woman. How I got the strength to fight him off is definitely divine intervention. Also, what are the chances of my running into the path of an off-duty police officer? I was looked after and am forever thankful. My attacker was a bad man – it frightens me to think of what could have been had my beautiful angels not given me such strength!

Some earth angels mysteriously appear and disappear and are impossible to trace afterwards, but others borrow the faces of friends, family or passing strangers, who may or may not be aware an angel is guiding them. Indeed, anyone who inspires you or lifts your spirits, or helps you grow and love more, is an angel, and this is the perfect place for this next story, sent to me by Gina.

Angel in the supermarket

It was Christmas Eve and I was doing a massive last-minute shop. This really wasn't like me. I'm normally a much more organised person and would have had everything ordered online but this year work had been manic and I just hadn't had the time. I was very much looking forward to Christmas as for the first time in five years my brother was coming with his wife and two children. It was going to be a real family Christmas.

I filled my shopping trolley sky high with Christmas food, treats and presents and then went to the checkout. It took a while queuing, paying and packing but I didn't mind – it was Christmas. I wheeled my trolley to the car and opened the boot and as I did I noticed this woman walking across the car park in my direction. It was a cold night and she looked freezing. She had a small child with her and I watched her take off her scarf, kneel down and wrap it around her child. As she walked on I noticed that she was limping. It was slow progress for her. I had recently recovered from a ski injury to my knee so I felt for her. She could only manage a few steps at a time and had to rest against the wall. It was Christmas so I decided to ask her if she was OK when she walked past.

She looked startled when I asked her and nodded rather unconvincingly. I still had a packet of herbal remedies in my pocket from my injury so I asked her if she would like to have them. When I handed them to her she said thank you and started to cry. She told me how incredibly kind I had been.

As she was speaking I really looked at her and saw how threadbare her clothes were. I looked at the shoes her child was wearing and thought about the warm boots my nieces would be wearing this Christmas. I can't explain why, as I was about to ruin Christmas for my family, but I found myself offering her the contents of my shopping trolley – all the food, treats and gifts in it. I could not believe what I was doing. The supermarket was going to close and there was no chance of my getting back inside and here I was giving away my Christmas to a complete stranger.

I'm really not normally the kind of person to do this sort of thing or act on impulse. I prefer to give to charity through my bank account, but something deep inside me was telling me what to do and deep down inside I knew I was doing the right thing.

At first the woman didn't want to take my gift but I was persistent and in the end she gave way. She could not stop crying and thanking me and told me I was an angel. She had indeed no food for Christmas and no presents for her little girl and this was a wonderful gift.

There have been many high points in my life – getting engaged, being promoted at work and losing twelve pounds – but nothing can ever compare to the feeling I had that night as I watched that woman walk away with my Christmas shopping. It was awesome to be a part of someone else's miracle.

And it was even more wonderful when I got home to find my brother and his wife and their children waiting for me with – you guessed it – a huge trolley full of shopping. Somewhere along the way we had got our wires crossed and they thought they had to buy all the Christmas food this year. If I had got home with my shopping too we would have had way too much food in the house. It felt like I was meant to meet that woman and give her the help she so clearly needed.

This story is a delightful reminder that it is not just angels around us who can save, heal or transform the lives of others – a spark of the divine can exist within each one of us.

For most of us today life has never been tougher. Our natural tendency during tough times is to withdraw from others, because we have our own concerns, fears and problems to deal with. The problem with withdrawal, though, is that it creates feelings of isolation and meaninglessness. Simple acts of kindness, however, can instantly connect us to others in deep and meaningful ways. Just a smile can light up someone's day, a kind word can brighten someone's spirits and a moment of consideration can bring a slice of heaven into the lives of others or be the bridge they need at that moment to help them through the day. Most of us don't realise that in the right time and place we can all be instruments of the divine and everything we say and do, however tiny or insignificant it may feel at the time, really has the potential to make others feel as if they have been touched by an angel.

Universally speaking, there's no such thing as a simple or small act of compassion or kindness. Every act of kindness creates a ripple effect which extends far beyond that act. That's the most amazing thing about kindness – when people are treated with kindness they are more likely to extend it to others. This lovely poem says it so eloquently ...

<u>*The Pebble*</u>

Drop a pebble in the water:
just a splash and it is gone,
But there are half-a-hundred ripples
circling on and on and on.
Spreading, spreading from the centre,
flowing on out to the sea.
And there is no way of telling
where the end is going to be.

Drop a word of cheer and kindness:
just a flash and it is gone;
But there are half-a-hundred ripples
circling on and on and on,

Touched by an Angel

Bearing hope and joy and comfort
on each splashing, dashing wave
Till you wouldn't believe the volume
of the one kind word you gave.

Drop a word of cheer and kindness:
in a minute you forget;
But there's gladness still a-swelling,
and there's joy a-circling yet,
And you've rolled a wave of comfort
whose sweet music can be heard
Over miles and miles of water
by just dropping one kind word.

James W. Foley, Jr

You have nothing to lose and everything to gain by being kind and loving. Love and kindness is the closest thing we have to experiencing heaven on earth. Someone inspired or uplifted by you may unknowingly pass those good feelings on to a friend; the friend may pass it on to a neighbour and so on and on. Your world will literally be transformed around you and for you by the unexpected ripples you have set in motion. Your kind word or deed may miraculously reach out to inspire countless other people.

It is in your spiritual DNA to treat everyone you meet with love, reverence and compassion. By being kind you are saving lives, conquering fear and making miracles happen, so why wait?

Let the angel inside you speak and you will witness your life as a series of heavenly encounters. See the angel in everyone and everything and you will always be in heaven. You see, whenever you feel love, compassion or kindness you are being an angel. You are spreading the word. You are overcoming the forces of darkness and death by drawing to earth the power of eternal light and truth.

You may not realise it but you can start saving and healing the world, one person at a time ... and it all begins with you.

CONCLUSION

Spreading your Wings

On earth, an angel's wings are inside.

Karen Goldman

It's amazing here, Molly: the love inside. You take it with you.

The evergreen movie *Ghost*, 1990

Angels – does it really matter how they save lives: as a feeling; in a dream; seeing them with spiritual or physical eyes; in the guise of a child; a beloved pet; an ordinary person. In whatever way we see, hear or feel them, does it matter as long as the message of love they bring is there – that we are not alone. Does it matter, as long as we are reminded that heaven isn't some faraway place we might go to when we die, but a place we can visit any time in our hearts? Attuning ourselves to heaven, we come to know our deep abiding connection to love, we become aware of our eternal power and an ocean inside us of boundless joy.

Spiritually-minded people have always thought for themselves and looked deep within themselves for answers, but today too many people have forgotten who they are. They think money, status, relationships or material possessions will save them or bring them comfort and fulfilment. They want joy and peace but they are searching outside themselves for their salvation. They do not realise that although we live in a physical world and have physical sensations, we have something more real, more powerful that is deep inside us.

You are and always will be a spark of the divine. Never forget that your real home is heaven and this life on earth is temporary. The key to your happiness, fulfilment and peace on earth is your spiritual growth. When you live every day seeing the world with spirit eyes you are already living an eternal life of truth. You are already spreading your wings as an aspiring angel.

Trust in that aspiring angel within you. It is that angel, and the feelings of love and compassion it evokes in your heart, which will rescue you. Believe in that angel and you are already, and always will be, saved.

I'll leave you for now with some angelic words to inspire and guide you and, as always, my favourite angel blessing to comfort and remind you.

People are like stained-glass windows. They sparkle and shine when the sun is out but when the darkness sets in their true beauty is only revealed if there is a light from within.

Elisabeth Kübler-Ross

Our greatest fear is not that we are inadequate, but that we are powerful beyond measure. It is our light, not our darkness, that frightens us. We ask ourselves, Who am I to be brilliant, gorgeous, handsome, talented and fabulous? Actually, who are you not to be?

You are a child of God. Your playing small does not serve the world. There is nothing enlightened about shrinking so that other people won't feel insecure around you. We were born to make manifest the glory of God within us. It is not just in some; it is in everyone. And, as we let our own light shine, we consciously give other people permission to do the same. As we are liberated from our fear, our presence automatically liberates others.

Marianne Williamson, *A Return to Love*

Angels around us, angels beside you, angels within you.
Angels are watching over you when times are good or stressed.
Their wings wrap gently around you, whispering you are loved and blessed.

Angel Blessing

About the Author

Theresa Cheung is the author of a variety of books including the *Sunday Times* bestsellers *An Angel Called My Name, An Angel on My Shoulder* and *Angel Babies*. She is also the author of the international bestseller *The Element Encyclopedia of 20,000 Dreams, The Element Encyclopedia of the Psychic World* and the top ten *Sunday Times* bestseller *An Angel Healed Me*, as well as *An Angel Changed My Life, How to See Your Angels* and *An Angel Spoke to Me*. Theresa's books have been translated into twenty different languages and her writing has featured in *Chat – It's Fate, Spirit & Destiny*, Prediction, Red and Prima magazines, as well as the *Daily Express, Daily Mail* and *Sunday Times Style*. In addition, Theresa has worked on books for Derek Acorah, Yvette Fielding, Tony Stockwell and Dr William Bloom. Born into a family of psychics and spiritualists, Theresa has been involved in the research of psychic phenomena for over twenty-five years since gaining a Masters from King's College, Cambridge. She has also been a student at the College of Psychic Studies in London.

Contact the Author

If you have an angel story, experience or insight and wish to share it with Theresa, she would love to hear from you. Please contact her care of Simon and Schuster, 1st Floor, 222 Gray's Inn Road, London WC1X 8HB or email her at: angeltalk710@aol.com